Praise for Danny Ko

"Drastic situations sometimes call for simple solutions. In these dire financial times, Danny Kofke offers just that."

—**Jeff Yeager**, Author of *The Cheapskate Next Door* and *The Ultimate Cheapskate's Road Map To True Riches*

"Danny Kofke's book, *A Simple Book of Financial Wisdom*, is a winner. It lays out in very simple terms a solid, wise approach to managing personal finances. It is particularly timely during these times of financial crisis. It offers hope and relief."

—**Juan Williams**, Journalist, Political Analyst for Fox News Channel and Author of *Muzzled: The Assault on Honest Debate*

"Danny Kofke doesn't just talk about finances, he practices what he preaches. *A Simple Book of Financial Wisdom* is a great read and so important in these times. Even more important is the message for children. In today's world the simple messages are the best."

—**Martha Zoller**, Host of Morning Talk with Martha Zoller and Former House of Representatives Candidate

"His lessons apply to anyone struggling to make ends meet on a modest income. He shows how relatively simple changes, starting with how you think about money, can lead to life-changing shifts."

—**Kimberly Palmer**, Credit Card and Personal Finance Expert at NerdWallet and Author of *Smart Mom, Rich Mom*

"If every American had read Danny Kofke's book before 2005, the housing collapse and economic recession of 2008 would have never happened. Danny's commonsense approach to a family's financial management is a recipe for peace of mind and a happy life."

—**Johnny Isakson**, Former U.S. Senator

"Danny Kofke has written a heartfelt and sensible book for those who want to accomplish more with their money. His wise advice is fun to read and will show you how to live wealthy no matter how much or how little you have."

—**Laura Adams**, Host of Money Girl podcast and Author of *Debt-Free Blueprint*

"Danny Kofke's book is a wakeup call. We are living in a day of financial crisis and this book offers you the financial skills to obtain freedom and help you plan a future that can bring greater security for you, your children and even your grand-children."

—**Dr. Marilyn Hickey**, President, Marilyn Hickey Ministries

"Danny Kofke is living proof that you can be happy and live well without pulling down a six-figure income."

—**Gerri Detweiler**, Personal Finance Expert and Author of *Reduce Debt, Reduce Stress*

"It's never too soon to begin learning important lessons about the vital areas of our lives. In this book, Danny Kofke, draws on his experience as a classroom teacher to deliver sound finan-cial principles in a way that will enable kids to learn, and par-ents to build wealth into a legacy and then a dynasty."

—**Jim Stovall**, Author of *The Millionaire Map*

"In an age where experts are everywhere, Danny Kofke lives what he has learned and believes. His engaging style makes this practical and hopeful book a valuable resource for families."

—**Ken Coleman**, Dave Ramsey Personality, Host of The Ken Coleman Show and Author of *The Proximity Principle: The Proven Strategy That Will Lead to a Career You Love*

"Many find managing their finances to be impossible. Danny's book will teach you what you need to do in order to accumu-late wealth even on a modest salary."

—**Tom Corley**, Bestselling and Award-Winning Author

"The majorities of Americans are not very financially literate and lack the ability to adequately plan for their retirement, as evidenced by most Americans over 65 being totally dependent on Social Security. In Danny Kofke's *A Bright Financial Future* he shares excellent real world tools to help parents better introduce their children to money and ways to handle it. I highly recommend reading it."

> —**Valentino Sabuco**, CFP®, AEP®, Executive Director and Publisher of The Financial Awareness Foundation

"*The Wealthy Teacher* is the perfect blueprint for financial success no matter what your salary. Danny Kofke's advice is spot on whether you want to save more money, reduce debt or better plan for retirement. You'll also love his many surprising insights—like how to fully own your home in just seven years, and why teachers are actually better investors than almost any other profession. I highly recommend this book!"

> —**Lynnette Khalfani-Cox**, The Money Coach and Author of the New York Times bestseller *Zero Debt*

Can I Borrow $400?

Can I Borrow $400?

How to Never Have to Ask this Question Again …
Win the Game of Financial Freedom!

DANNY KOFKE

W
Wyatt-MacKenzie Publishing
DEADWOOD, OREGON

Can I Borrow $400?

How to Never Have to Ask this Question Again ...
Win the Game of Financial Freedom!

Danny Kofke

ISBN: 978-1-942545-94-1

The publisher and editors do not assume any legal responsibility for errors, omissions or claims, nor do they provide any warranty, expressed or implied, with respect to information published. Although the author has made every effort to ensure that the information in this book was correct at press time, the author and publisher do not assume and hereby disclaim any liability to any party for any loss, damage, or disruption caused by errors or omissions, whether such errors or omissions result from negligence, accident, or any other cause.

Wyatt-MacKenzie Publishing
DEADWOOD, OREGON

Wyatt-MacKenzie Publishing, Inc.
www.WyattMacKenzie.com
Contact us: info@wyattmackenzie.com

TABLE OF CONTENTS

Author's Note

April 2, 2020

For many, poor financial decision-making directly leads to money issues. During normal times, most people get themselves into financial trouble because of ill-advised money moves. That all changed with COVID-19. Many people who made good financial decisions were, and continue to be, negatively impacted. Just last week Congress passed a stimulus plan to help with this. This money will help, but I am not sure if it will be enough.

Even though times are extremely scary right now, I feel confident we will make it through this. In fact, since I am an optimistic person, I believe many of us can become better at handling our money when this all passes.

Like other tragic times in our history, the Coronavirus has made us focus on what is truly important—our health and the ones we love. Most everything else seems pretty meaningless right now. In addition, this virus has also shown how little control we truly have This is why it is so important to control those things that we *can*—handling our finances.

What Finances To Focus On During A Global Crisis

Unfortunately, some of you are still feeling the financial effects caused by this pandemic and don't know what to focus on. With so many bills due, it can be overwhelming. If you are in this situation, I encourage you to focus on the following four items before anything else:

1. Housing/Utilities

One of our basic needs is shelter, so housing and utilities must be taken care of first. When I say utilities, I mean lights, water and electricity. Cable does not count. Since many have to work from home (and most school-age children are doing school from home), internet can be included here as well.

2. Food

This is another of our basic needs. However, when times are tough, we are not looking at eating the most expensive meals. I am all for staying healthy, but if you have lost income and money is tight look at how to get the most bang for your bucks.

3. Transportation

This may not be a necessity for all, but if you need transportation to earn an income it is. With some public transportation reducing hours of operation or shutting down altogether, having the means to travel to make money is a must.

4. Health Insurance

I hope you didn't have any medical issues occur due to this virus, but the spread showed why it is so important to have health insurance. Never go without this important protection! If you happened to lose your health insurance because of job loss, here are some places you can look to obtain it:

- Obamacare Exchanges

  If you have lost your employer-based health insurance, you can look into Affordable Care Act policies by visiting **www.healthcare.gov.** There is only 60-day window to enroll in one of these policies after an individual's employer coverage ends. These plans can be costly but the government gives subsidies for lower and middle income individuals. People who make up to $50,000 a year and families of four with earnings up to $103,000 a year usually qualify for some sort of financial help.

· Medicaid
If you find yourself suddenly unemployed, you may qualify for health care coverage through Medicaid. Many states have expanded eligibility for Medicaid. Individuals who make around $17,500 or less this year and families of four earning less than $431,150 are typically able to sign up. You can learn more here: https://www.healthcare.gov/medicaid-chip/medicaid-expansion-and-you/

· COBRA
COBRA (the Consolidated Omnibus Budget Reconciliation Act of 1985) allows individuals to keep their job-based health insurance coverage for up to 18 month after they lose their job. This can be pretty expensive but is also an option.

Once this crisis passes and things get back to normal, other categories can slowly be integrated back into life (that is assuming your financial situation allows for it). But, if you are out of work and living on a limited income, focus on these four needs before anything else!

COVID-19 — 10 Financial Steps To Take Right Now

I know we still have some tough times ahead, but we will weather this storm. Here are some actions we can take in this midst of, and after, this pandemic has passed:

Build/Grow Your Emergency Fund
If you find yourself lucky enough to still be collecting a paycheck, you should try to save as much as possible in case you find

yourself out of work in the future. This holds true in normal times as well but has really become urgent in these times. In this book, I discuss The Game of Financial Freedom—this game lists the exact levels you need to pass before moving on to the next. This game is discussed in chapter three. We start saving money once we reach level five when we save one month of expenses in a savings account. Once this is accomplished, we proceed to level six and start investing for retirement. The Game of Financial Freedom is to be followed during times of normalcy—we are definitely not in normal times right now. Since this is the case, I advise you to tweak the game a bit and, in level five, I want you to save **six** months of living expenses if possible (if not, save as much as you can). This money is to be placed in a savings account. It is quite possible the financial consequences of COVID-19 will last longer than the virus itself. Saving as much money as possible will help greatly in case this happens.

With many places of entertainment closed, there might be less temptations to spend your money. If you have filed your taxes this year, your refund can go in your savings account. In addition, most of us will be getting stimulus checks which can go into your savings account. While the goal is to save at least six months of living expenses, some margin is better than none.

See If You Can Skip Payments On Some Of Your Loans

To help consumers during these tough times, some banks and credit card companies are offering help such as waived fees and, in some cases, no interest due on credit cards. In addition, the federal government has ordered mortgage companies to allow individuals who have either lost their job or income due to the Coronavirus to make reduced payments and, in some cases, skip payments altogether. To qualify, one has to have suffered some sort of financial hardship related to the virus that makes him unable to meet his basic living expenses. This includes losing the ability to work due to illness or job loss. However, if you are in this situation, you can't just stop paying these bills! You need to call your lender or the company you owe this debt to. For example, if you are having trouble making your mortgage payment due to COVID-19, you need to call the company you send your mortgage payment to every month. Let them know you are having difficulty making your monthly payment due to the Coronavirus and need to make reduced payments or skip them entirely for a period of time. If you decide to skip payments, you will still owe the lender this money eventually—it doesn't just get erased. The most likely outcome is these missed payments will be tacked on to the end of your loan. So let's say you currently have ten years left on your mortgage (120 months). If you were able to skip your payments for six months, this loan will be paid off in 126 months.

Make sure you get any type of loan modifications in writing. If you are able to restructure any of your loans, you can use this saved money and build your emergency fund.

Revisit Your Budget

In times of an emergency, we need to take a deeper look at our budgets and what we are spending money on. If you find yourself out of work, many things can be eliminated from your normal monthly budget. Remember, we focus on housing, food, health insurance and transportation first. In desperate times, almost everything else is frivolous. Cable television, brand new smart phones, and gym memberships can be eliminated for the time being. Use this money to build up your savings. This will not be forever—things will get back to normal and you can add these items back. Take a look at your latest bank and credit card statements and see if there are some items that can temporarily be cut out. Every dollar counts!

Find Any Job You Can

The Coronavirus Rescue Package passed by Congress has enabled almost anyone who has lost income due to the Coronavirus to qualify for unemployment benefits. This is a great thing! However, I would also encourage anyone struggling financially to look for some sort of employment anywhere. There are many places looking for workers. If you are looking for employment, here are some industries that may be hiring:

- Shipping and Delivery Companies
- Online Learning Companies
- Grocery Stores and Delivery Services
- Remote Meeting and Communication Companies

Keep in mind this may not (and probably is not) your dream job. However, when times are tough, sometimes you just have to put one foot in front of the other and just keep moving. A few years ago, I left teaching and was working for a company that offered financial literacy to churches across the country. I was laid-off towards the end of September. I figured I would just get back into teaching, but September is probably the worst time of year to look for a teaching job. While waiting for a teaching position to become available, I worked in a call center for a company that provided insurance benefits to school systems. I had to leave my house at 5:00 am and would not get home until after 8:00 pm most evenings since it was a 140-mile roundtrip. I did enjoy this, but being in the car almost four hours every workday was not ideal. However, this allowed me to make money until I found a school that was hiring a special education teacher closer to my home.

Take Advantage Of Low Interest Rates

The Federal Reserve recently slashed its rates to almost zero. This means that interest rates on some loans are very low. Take a look at refinancing them. Doing so could help you save money over time. In addition, you could possibly reduce the amount of money you are currently paying by extending the term of the loan. While this should be the **LAST** option, it can help in the short term. While I have never given advice to extend the length of a loan (especially in a book about becoming debt free), I understand these are different times than many of us have ever faced.

Temporarily Pause Contributing To Your Retirement Account

If you are currently putting money aside for retirement, it might be time to stop this until things get back to normal. It is very important to set money aside for the future but, if you are having trouble making ends meet this week, it is pretty foolish to worry about 30 years down the road. When times are tough, cash is definitely king. Instead of investing for the long-term, we need to focus on the short-term. Once this passes, you can start contributing again.

Don't Sell Investments Because You Are Afraid

In the Game of Financial Freedom, you begin investing for retirement in level six. This comes after saving one month of expenses which, as I mentioned above, I want you to increase to at least six months' worth of expenses. After you do this, you can begin investing for retirement.

You may already have money in a retirement account. Well, after seeing it grow for over ten years, the month of March 2020 changed all that. In fact, here are some very depressing statistics:

- The Dow closed down 13.74% in March, notching its worst month since October 2008.

- The Dow closed down -23.2% for the quarter, its worst since the fourth quarter of 1987. It was the Dow's worst first quarter ever.

- The Dow is 25.88% below its intraday all-time high of 29,568.57 from Feb 12.

- The S&P closed down 1.6% for its second negative day in three, closing up or down more than 1% every day in March with the exception of March 19.

- The S&P closed down 12.51% over the month of March, its worst month since October 2008.

- The index closed down 20% for the first quarter, its worst quarter since the fourth quarter of 2008, when the S&P 500 lost 22.56%. It was the S&P 500's worst first quarter ever.

- Sectors: 10 out of 11 sectors were negative today led by Utilities down 4.02%.

- Nine out of 11 sectors closed down at least 20% below their 52-week high closes with the exception of Health Care and Staples. (a)

Yes, pretty scary! If you are keeping track of your investments, this is not fun to look at. It can be very stressful to watch the value of your retirement account free fall. However, we need to remember this is only temporary. Money invested for retirement should not be needed for at least five years. In fact, if you are not looking to retire for another 20 years, this is actually a **GREAT** time to be buying stocks and mutual funds since they are on sale. When we look over the course of time and average annual returns, the stock market grows and investments increase in value.

The two major stock indexes (mentioned above) are the Dow and the S&P 500. The Dow refers to the Dow Jones Industrial Average (DJIA). It is a stock market index that shows how 30 large publicly owned companies based in the United States have traded during a standard trading session in the stock market.

It is often used to measure the United States industry. The S&P 500 (the Standard and Poor's 500 Index) is an index of 500 stocks chosen for market size, liquidity, and industry grouping, among other factors. The S&P 500 is designed to be a leading indicator of U.S. stocks.

Basically, these two stock indexes provide a basis for how strong the U.S. stock market is. If you judge stocks by these two indexes, they have done pretty well over the course of time. The Dow averaged 7.75% annual growth from 1921 to 2019. (b) The average annual return of the S&P 500 since its start in 1926 through the year 2018 is around 10%. (c) Now that is not saying that stocks grow this amount every year; rather, it is their average. Some years the market is up 15 percent and other years it is down 20 percent; however, the average annual growth when we look at both indexes is over 7%. This time frame encompassed a World War, the Great Depression, the tragedy of 9/11, the housing crisis of 2008 and countless other major events.

Do I (or anyone else for that matter) have any idea what the market is going to do next? Absolutely not! But, based on past performance, I feel okay to leave the money I have invested alone. I am not guaranteed any growth at all, but since I look at past performance as my guide, I don't get too freaked out when the market dips. Let's say you see a sweater at Macy's that costs $50. This is too much for you so you choose not to buy it. Two weeks later it goes on sale for half off. At this price, you might consider buying it. That is the way I view the stock market. When it's down, I look at it like I'm buying stocks and mutual funds on sale. I remember this is not the first time the market has dropped and it definitely won't be the last.

Have Emergency Plans In Place

I have what I call my Legacy File in my firebox. This term is something I learned from Dave Ramsey's book *The Legacy Journey: A Radical View of Biblical Wealth and Generosity.* This file basically contains all of our family's important documents in one large envelope. This ensures we can find all of this information at a moment's notice. I talk to my wife all the time about our finances, but she doesn't always remember what I said. This file is great for us. If something were to happen to me, she could look in one place and have all of this information. In addition, if we had to evacuate (we have had to before because of a tornado warning), we can just grab this file, bring it with us, and we will have all the information we need if we had to start over. I know it doesn't sound very optimistic, but it actually helps us sleep more soundly.

Here is what is included in our Legacy File:

Debit/Credit Card Copy

Driver's License Copy

Pay Stub

Monthly Budget

Phone Numbers

Contact List

Financial Information

Bank Account Information

Email Information

Birth Certificates

Social Security Cards

Passports

Marriage Certificate

Auto Insurance

Homeowner's Insurance

Health Insurance

Life Insurance

Power of Attorney

Wills

Advance Directive for Health Care

Tax Return (Current Year)

Retirement Account Information

Pension Info

Car Titles

Mortgage Information

In addition to having this information at our house, I also made a copy of its contents and gave it to my mom. This way, if something happened to our file, we have a back-up that we can easily get our hands on. It took me the good part of a Saturday afternoon to gather all of this information, but a few hours is a small price to pay to have all of this in one place for the rest of our lives.

Keep Some Cash Handy

I am not one to panic too much and feel that money in bank account is safe but it is important to have some cash readily available just in case we have a full-scale shutdown. Now, I'm not saying to bury thousands of dollars in your backyard but having $200-$300 in cash will never hurt.

Keeping cash on hand is good at any time—not just because of COVID-19. I also recommend keeping cash in your vehicle. I realized the importance of this a few years ago. My family and I were heading to a cabin in the Tennessee mountains as a winter storm was on the way. We were scheduled to arrive a few hours ahead of it and stopped to get fuel for our car. Well, the debit/credit card reader was not working due to ice. Good thing we had cash hidden in the car to pay for our fuel.

Take A Deep Breath—This Will Pass

Yes, this is easier said than done. As I write this, school has been closed for the remainder of this school year. Figures for last week were just released and a record 6.6 million people filed for unemployment benefits. I can't even watch sports as a distraction (that Netflix subscription is worth a lot more than what I am paying for it right now) and all that is on the news is pretty scary. However, I am controlling what I can, and making sure I take the medical community's advice and stay home as much as possible. In addition, I am still exercising daily—this helps keep me somewhat balance. As frightening as this is, I do not want to panic since panic leads to irrational thinking which can compound into making poor decisions.

COVID-19 is extremely scary and, at this point, no one knows how long it will last and how bad it could get. However, we will get through this. So, I am taking the time to focus on what is really important—the health of my family and myself.

Preface

"Everybody has a plan until they get punched in the mouth."

MIKE TYSON

Recently my wife, Tracy, had to have surgery to remove cancerous skin from her forehead (thank goodness it was nothing major and the dermatologist caught it before it became something more serious). We have good health insurance so figured she would just have a co-pay of maybe a hundred bucks or so. Well, upon arriving at the doctor's office, Tracy was told she had to pay $750! Yes, you read that correctly. Yikes.

Don't get me wrong, we were not overly thrilled about this, but it really did not change our lives. Since we have a one-year emergency fund in place, she paid this amount, got the cancerous skin removed, and we moved on with life. However, this got me thinking: how many others would feel the same way? Well, as it turns out, only 60% of Americans could cover a **$400** unexpected expense! (a)

Because this is the case regarding just a $400 expense, I am sure even fewer could cover a more costly one. This has to change! Many of us are one slip away from financial disaster. The main reason for this is the amount of debt we have. In fact, almost 30% have more credit card debt than savings. (b)

The following is a fictional story but, unfortunately, I bet it can relate to some of you.

An American Story

John and Julie started off their marriage like a typical American couple. They met at work and fell in love quickly. They both graduated from college with student loan debt. In fact, they each carried the average balance: over $37,000. (c)

Julie is a nurse and makes $36,000 a year. John is a teacher and his annual salary is $35,000. Think about this for a minute. They each earn less than they owe. If Julie and John did not have anything taken out of their pay (including taxes which would lead to a lot more trouble) they could work an entire year and still not be able to pay off their student loan debt! Even though they both majored in fields that do not pay large salaries, they didn't really think about this when obtaining their student loans.

John was so in love with Julie and wanted to make their engagement as special as possible. He had only $500 in savings when they started getting serious. Shortly after that, he knew she was the one. Despite having little in his bank account, he bought a $10,000 engagement ring. He obtained a store credit card from a jewelry store in the mall and put the entire cost of the ring on that. The payment was interest-free for five years, and he figured he would easily pay it off by then. The minimum monthly payments were only $100 and John figured once they got married, they would combine their salaries and be able to pay extra towards the balance.

Their engagement was magical. Julie always talked about how her favorite place to visit was Disney World. Yep, you guessed it: John planned a magical day at The Magic Kingdom. In fact, John got down on one knee in front of Cinderella's castle right as the fireworks were going off. Yes, it was like a story book! However, because he didn't have the money upfront to pay for this special day, it all went on the Visa card.

After the engagement, John and Julie began planning for the big day. They did discuss keeping the costs down and possibly having a small ceremony, but as they were both in careers that revolve around people, they had many guests who *needed* to come to their wedding. Julie's parents agreed to pay for half the cost of this special day, but John and Julie had to pay for the rest of it. As fate would have it, the cost was the average price a couple spends on their wedding today: over $44,000! (d)

While this was a steep price, John and Julie felt it was worth it. Everyone had so much fun, and they started off their marriage on the right track (at least they thought so at the time). The following day, they flew off to Mexico for a week-long honeymoon spent in the sun. It was one of the best weeks of their lives.

After the honeymoon, they decided to rent a small apartment. This was going to be temporary because they had dreams of buying a starter home. However, one month later, the credit card bills (along with the added stress) started to arrive. Their wedding expenses alone totaled more than what they earned in a year after taxes and insurance were deducted from their paychecks (this included the cost of the engagement ring, their part of the wedding costs, and the honeymoon). While it sounded like a good idea at the time, they now began to wonder if it was really worth it. When they added their student loan debt to the credit card debt, they barely had enough to cover their current living expenses, let alone a much more costly mortgage payment. Even though they both loved kids and wanted a large family, they didn't see how it would be possible to support even one child. Once the honeymoon ended, it seemed like the fun did, too.

Most people would agree that this is not a great way to start off a marriage. Unfortunately, many of us fall into this debt trap and begin our lives already behind the eight ball. I hope your story is not like John and Julie's but if it is (or you know someone whose life is like theirs) I have some great news for you: life allows us to learn from our mistakes and make a change in the right direction. It will take some work and sacrifice, but this book will show you how it can be done. You can march toward debt freedom and live a wealthy life!

Wealthy Life Question

Can you relate to John and Julie? If so, how? If not, how is your situation different?

Introduction

*"Everyone thinks about changing the world but
no one thinks of changing himself."*

LEO TOLSTOY

My Debt Story

I knew I wanted to be a teacher after being taught by Mr. Stutzke in 9th grade. He taught Civics and was just one of those special teachers that many of us have had (if you are a teacher reading this, you probably had that special teacher who led you into the profession). Mr. Stutzke was that teacher for me. Even though I was in his class more than 25 years ago, I still remember his motto: "Stand and Deliver." Anytime a student had something to say, she had to stand by her desk and say it. Looking back now, I had no clue how this would help prepare me for my future. Like most teenagers, I was nervous to get up in front of the room and speak to the class. This practice that Mr. Stutzke employed forced us to speak in front of the class in a less threatening way. As an adult, I have presented in rooms full of hundreds of people, and I am not ever nervous. I have Mr. Stutzke to thank for helping me with this!

Most would agree that teachers are not paid a large salary, especially early in their careers. Because I knew I wanted to become a teacher at a fairly young age, I realized I would have to be very careful with my money or marry someone who made more. Option B went out the window when I met my wife, Tracy!

I showed up for my student teaching assignment (many colleges have education majors intern for one semester in their chosen subject) and immediately fell for a first grade teacher: Tracy. She was a natural-born teacher and just amazing. It was a fast courtship, and we were engaged December of that year, married the following June, and living and teaching in another country on the one-year anniversary of the day we met! With two daughters of our own now, I can clearly see why her parents were a little worried that she was rushing into this; but 19 years later, we are still going strong.

The Planning Begins

I guess you could say my experience with debt—or a lack of it—began when I was a child. My mother, father, brother, and I lived in a small two-bedroom, one-bathroom house until I was in sixth grade. My parents both felt strongly about having my mom be a stay-at-home mom and had to make certain lifestyle choices to make that a reality. Even though my dad did not make a lot of money, we never felt like we did not have what we wanted. As I got older, I realized how they were able to do this: they had no debt except the mortgage. When you get to pay yourself rather than someone else, your salary goes a lot farther.

Because of my upbringing, I really wanted Tracy to be able to stay home when we had children. Since we would be living off my teacher's salary of around $40,000 a year, we knew we had to be very careful to make this happen. We spent the beginning years of our marriage building up savings and eliminating debt to make our goal a reality.

We faced our first major choice when purchasing a car. We had planned on using some of our savings to put a down payment on two cars, one for each of us. Everyone has to have a car, right? Well, we spent our first two years of marriage living and teaching in Krakow, Poland, and did not have a car. Going for two years without having even one car made us rethink this belief. What if we could get by with only one automobile? That would help us achieve our goal of having Tracy stay home. We decided to try this approach and purchased one car for us to share.

Sharing a car was not always easy. We taught at separate schools. The plan most of the time was for me to drop Tracy off at her school and then drive to mine. This was not too difficult, as both of our schools were within a five-mile radius of our house. However, there were days when Tracy had a meeting at another location after school and needed the car. What to do then? Well, because we lived about two miles from my school, I would ride my bike to work. Yes, you read that correctly. I was the only teacher who parked his bike at the bike rack. There were some who made fun of me for this. I heard comments like, "Get off your wallet, Danny" or "Live a little." This is when I learned another valuable lesson: if people who have no money are making fun of you, keep doing what you are doing! I know this is much easier said than done, but it is so true. If I went to a personal trainer and he weighed 400 pounds and smoked 2 packs of cigarettes a day, I would do the complete opposite of what he told me to do unless I wanted to look like him. Why let people who are deeply in debt dictate how you spend money unless you want to end up like them: in debt?

Because we had only one car, we paid extra money on this loan each month. We pretended like we had two car payments and paid the entire amount toward our one car. This enabled us to pay it off in two years! I am proud to write that I drove this car for 16 and a half years. I literally drove it until it died. One morning on my way to work it just died. I was fortunate enough to make it to a parking lot and had to have it towed to a car dealership to use as a trade-in. I had not had a car payment for 176 months. The average monthly new car payment is $530. (a)

So, continuing to drive this same car for more than 16 years enabled me to save over $93,000!!!!!

Another major decision we faced was buying a house. The conventional wisdom at this time was to qualify for as much as possible and buy as much house as your lender said you could afford. However, this strategy would work against our goal of Tracy being able to stay home. We shopped around and soon found a beautiful two-bedroom home priced way below the amount for which we qualified. We quickly signed on the dotted line, and within two months of moving home from Poland, we had a car and a house. Our American Dream had begun.

The Planning Pays Off

Over the next two years, Tracy and I continued to follow our plan. On May 26th, 2004, we welcomed our daughter, Ava, to our family. One month later, the car was paid off. This positioned us to have Tracy stay home with her.

In 2007, another daughter, Ella, arrived. Even though I was making around $42,000 a year teaching, we were able to live comfortably. Now granted, we didn't drive fancy cars or dine at expensive restaurants, but we had the freedom to pursue our desires: me to teach and Tracy to stay home and raise Ava and Ella. Through sound planning and living below our means, Tracy was able to stay home full-time a total of eight years.

Despite living off my teacher's salary alone during that time, we have no debt except our mortgage, are on track to retire with a sizable nest egg, have a one-year emergency fund in place, and, most importantly, live wealthy lives on less. Yes, we made what some would call sacrifices but we never really looked at it like that. My dream was to be a teacher and Tracy's was to be a stay-at-home mom. Through careful planning and decision making, we were able to achieve both of these goals. Where others looked at our decisions as sacrifices, we viewed them as stepping stones on the path to achieving some of our hopes and dreams. Once we were able to realize these dreams, we did not want to change. Accumulating debt would have required us to so.

Becoming an Author

Shortly after getting married, some of my colleagues noticed how Tracy and I lived differently from many. Before Ava was born, some even suggested that I write a book sharing how we did this. I didn't really give it much thought until a November weekend in 2005. Tracy and Ava had gone to visit her sister, and I was home alone. God put a vision in my head to sit down and start writing. It is the only explanation I have. I followed this promptly, and some amazing things have happened.

I began to write, and after a few months, had it all on paper. I really had no intention of doing anything with this. I just thought it was neat to have my thoughts down to share with my family and some friends. One person suggested I try and publish it. I did some research and submitted it to a few publishers. One of them—a self-publishing service—accepted it with a clause: I would have to pay a fee of almost $4,000 for assistance having it published! Tracy and I discussed and prayed about this and decided it was worth the risk. In October of 2007, *How To Survive (and perhaps thrive) On A Teacher's Salary* was released.

This book was the start of an amazing ride. Fast-forward fifteen years since I started writing and my life has drastically changed because of this book. I have written three other books, all traditionally published (without a fee!): *The Wealthy Teacher: Lessons For Prospering On A School Teacher's Salary, A Bright Financial Future: Teaching Kids About Money Pre-K through College for Life-Long Success* and *A Simple Book of Financial Wisdom: Teach Yourself (and Your Kids) How to Live Wealthy with Little Money.* In addition, my daughter, Ava, was offered a publishing contract for her own book in September 2014 titled *The Financial Angel: What All Kids Should Know About Money.*

These books have led me to be interviewed on television more than 50 times and counting. Some were on national shows such as The CBS Early Show, Fox & Friends, CNN's Newsroom, Fox Business Network's The Willis Report, HLN's Weekend Express, The 700 Club, The Clark Howard Show, and MSNBC Live. I have also been interviewed on more than 650 radio shows and featured in numerous publications such as USA Today, Consumer Reports, Yahoo.com, Money Magazine, Bankrate.com, Instructor Magazine, The Atlanta Journal Constitution, Woman's Day, and The Wall Street Journal.

Saving the best for last, being an author has enabled me to help thousands of people manage their money better, something I feel I was put on Earth to do! If Tracy and I had a lot of debt, I would not have been able to take advantage of the offer to write my first book because I would not have had any money. God gives opportunities to us when we manage well what we have. It seems like the less debt I had, the more opportunities I was presented with.

Let's Go

Okay, you know my story, and now it is time for you to change yours. In the following pages, I will lay out a plan that will enable you to pay off your debt and start living a wealthy life. A wealthy life is being able to do exactly what you have been put on earth to do, regardless of the cost or income potential. The great thing about it is, if Tracy and I can do it, you can, too.

Wealthy Life Question

After reading my story, what do you feel is the most important thing Tracy and I did to manage our debt?

Chapter 1

Why Do We Have Debt

One pretends to be rich, yet has nothing;
another pretends to be poor, yet has great wealth.

PROVERBS 13:7

Before we get into some of the reasons that many of us find ourselves with little or no money at the end of the month, take a look at some statistics:

As of December 2019, the average U.S. household debt picture looked like this:

Average revolving* credit card debt: $7,104

Average mortgage debt: $192,618

Average student loan debt: $46,679

carried month to month

In total, American consumers owe:

$14.15 trillion in debt

$466.2 billion in revolving credit card debt

$9.56 trillion in mortgages

$1.51 trillion in student loans (a)

It is very difficult to get ahead financially when you owe others money and have nothing saved.

The Debt Fallacy

Unfortunately, our very own economy (if you are a U.S. citizen) is built on debt. As I write this, our national debt is over $23 trillion. (b)

To put this amount into perspective, if you were born on the same day that Jesus was and spent $1 million every day until today, you would not have spent $1 trillion. Our debt is over $23 trillion! (c)

In fact, if you spent one dollar per second, in a day you would spend $86,400. Over the course of a year, your spending would come to more than $31.5 million. At that rate of spending, it would take you more than 32,000 years to spend one trillion dollars. (d)

I am just pointing out what many of you know. In fact, our government is representative of us. It is of the people, by the people, for the people. Broke people have elected representatives just like them.

Unfortunately, like the people we elect, we get accustomed to taking on more and more debt. I don't know about you, but I get offers every week from a credit card company wanting me to become a "valuable" card holder. With this constant bombardment, it is actually kind of surprising we are not in worse financial shape. However, what these very same special offers don't point out is that once we take on debt, we no longer are in control of our time and effort. We now owe someone money and, thus, have to use our manpower and time to earn this money only to turn right back around and pay it to someone else. In addition, oftentimes interest (sometimes lots of it) is added to this amount!

You Are Already Rich

You might be in a profession that doesn't pay well but let's take a look at your salary compared to the world at large. By global standards:

- If you make $37,000 a year you are in the top 4% of wage earners.
- If you make $50,000 or more a year you are in the top 1%. (e)

In fact, if you live in America (generally speaking—I know there are some exceptions), you have a much richer life than almost anyone else living in the world. The problem is we tend to focus on our circle of friends and compare what we don't have to what they do. We think it is a tragedy when we can't get a signal on our cell phone yet thousands of people will go to sleep hungry tonight. Looking at the bigger picture can help us greatly. Unfortunately, we usually compare ourselves to our current situation rather than looking at the bigger picture.

I know that how much we make and how "rich" we feel is based on our own personal perspective. However, by taking a look at the numbers, I hope we realize that most people have it so much better than countless others. In fact, most of us don't have an income problem: we have an outgo one.

So what are some of the reasons we get into trouble with money? Let's take a look.

Lack of Contentment

Many of us are rich but we don't feel like it. We look at others and wish we had what they had. Here are some truths about losing contentment:

- The more we shop, the more we spend.
- The more we watch television, the more we spend.
- The more time we spend looking through catalogs, the more we spend.
- The more we read magazine ads, the more we spend.
- The more time we spend surfing the web, the more we spend.
- The more we spend looking at our "friends'" social media posts, the more we spend.

I know these seem like a no-brainer but many of us don't give these truths much thought. Madison Avenue spends billions of dollars every year to entice us to part with our money, but it really hit home for me recently at how hard they try. I was watching The World Series and a Christmas commercial came on. It was not even Halloween yet! In fact, there are estimates that most Americans are exposed to 4,000-10,000 ads every day! (f)

To illustrate the power of ads a little more, read the following story:

A large manufacturing firm decided to open a new assembly plant in an underdeveloped Latin American country because labor was cheap and plentiful. The plant was successfully opened and the operation was progressing smoothly—until the first paycheck. The next day, none of the villagers reported for work. Management waited ... one, two, three days. Still no villagers came to work. The plant manager went to see the village chief to find out the problem. "Why should we continue to work?" the chief asked in response to the manager's inquiry. "We are satisfied. We have already earned all the money we need to live on." The plant stood idle for almost a month. Then someone came up with the idea of distributing Sears catalogs to all the villagers. Reading the catalogs created new needs in the lives of the villagers. Since that time, there has not been an unemployment problem.

I know I can relate to that. Sometimes ignorance can be bliss. Try to find contentment in what you have and you won't feel like you are lacking in anything. A great saying to help with this is, "Want what you have and you will always have what you want." Makes perfect sense on paper but then we are bombarded by advertisements and our emotions kick in and we want what others have, not just what we already have. Once we realize we could have more, many of us automatically want more. The key is to try and find a level of contentment so that you do not have to compare yourself to others and how much more "stuff" they have compared to you.

SCARY DEBT STATISTIC

In a survey The Federal Reserve Board con-ducted, The Fed asked respondents how they would pay for a $400 emergency. 47% said they would either cover the expense by borrowing or selling something. If they could not borrow or sell something, they could not come up with this $400.

We Don't Have Goals or a Plan

Another reason people don't handle money well is that they have not set goals and, thus, do not have a plan. Benjamin Franklin said, "If you fail to plan, you are planning to fail." This is why almost one-fourth of us have nothing saved. If you don't have a destination in mind, it is hard to get there.

I am directionally challenged. If I were to drive from Georgia to Florida, I would need a GPS device to help me get there. With-out it, I might end up in North Carolina! Using a GPS device enables me to see checkpoints along the way to ensure I am heading in the correct direction. The same holds true with saving money: we first need a plan. Let's say your goal is to have $6,000 in your savings account by this time next year. Now we have a goal and can work on achieving it. We divide $6,000 by 12 months to establish a monthly goal. We can easily keep track of this monthly goal. We now know what we need at each month to ensure we achieve the goal. We must then come up with a plan of attack to save $500 each month.

We first came up with a goal. Then we looked at a way to track progress. Finally, we came up with a plan that would help us achieve this goal. Without having these checkpoints in place, it would be very difficult to save money because we would not clearly see our progress.

We Try To Keep Up With The Wrong People

A final reason people many are broke is that they try to emulate others. I know some who even try to impress people they don't know! They buy really expensive cars they truly cannot afford to impress someone next to them at a red light. They may get a look of jealousy from that person but will probably never even see them again. Trying to impress others is a recipe for disaster.

Warren Buffett is a perfect example of someone who doesn't try to keep up with others nor cares about what they think about him. He is ranked among the richest people in the world yet lives the same way he lived before he had billions of dollars. He still resides in the same house he bought in 1958 for $31,500. He is also known for his simple tastes like McDonald's hamburgers and Cherry Coke.

Mr. Buffett often says, "The first rule of investing is don't lose money; the second rule is don't forget Rule No. 1." This carries over into his personal life as well. Despite having a net worth over $60 billion, he earns a base salary of $100,000 a year from Berkshire Hathaway. Because he has simple tastes, he is able to easily live off this salary.

In an interview, Mr. Buffett described success as this:

"Success is really doing what you love and doing it well. It's as simple as that. Really getting to do what you love to do every day— that's really the ultimate luxury ... your standard of living is not equal to your cost of living." (g)

WOW! I can relate to this. I did not get into teaching to make a lot of money. I got into teaching because I had a passion for helping others. Over time, this passion prompted me to write books which led to opportunities to teach others how to manage money. Some days are more difficult than others and it is not all rainbows and butterflies, but I am doing exactly what I feel called to do. That is definitely something that you cannot put a price tag on.

Mr. Buffett is happy with what he has. He is not interested in a bigger house or a newer car. He really could care less about what his neighbors have. The thing is, unless you are the wealthiest person on Earth, there will always be someone with more. If you are continuously looking to live up to others, you will find yourself broke. It doesn't matter how much you have coming in: if you spend more than you earn, you won't have any money. This holds true whether you make $10,000, $100,000 or even $1,000,000 a year.

To further illustrate this, what do 50 Cent, Tom Petty, Don Johnson, and our current President, Donald Trump, all have in common? Even though they all made a lot of money, they all ended up making unwise choices with it. (h,i,j,k,)

They may have lost contentment, didn't have a plan, or tried to keep up with others (or maybe all three), and as a result found themselves out of money.

Try at all costs to avoid those three things, and you will position yourself to win with money.

Money Issues Are Mostly Due To Behavior, Not Math

Most of us can figure out how much interest we will be paying if we get into debt; it is basic eighth-grade math. Yet, millions still choose to sign up for debt. Why is this? Obviously, it is not the math! For most of us, money problems center around our behavior.

To win with money, we need to look to others who have had success and follow their habits. While many of us think fancy cars and big houses are the signs of success, the complete opposite is the truth. Here are some common characteristics of millionaires:

- Millionaires live frugally.
- Millionaires drive used (not new) cars.
- Millionaires buy their used cars and do not lease them.
- Millionaires live in houses below what they could afford to live in.

The majority of self-made millionaires budget and track **every** penny. (l)

Notice there is no mention of taking on debt! I know some did so to get an education and/or grow a business (we will get into the different kinds of debt in a bit) but living below your means is a tried and true formula for financial success.

Like we discussed before, if more goes out than comes in, you will eventually find yourself with no money. If you make $1,000,000 but spend $1,000,001 this principle still applies.

I know it sounds pretty basic. So why do so many of us find ourselves in debt? It goes back to contentment. As Americans, we live in one of the richest nations on Earth. Despite that, many of us are unhappy. In fact, according to a recent study, more than 70% of workers are miserable in their jobs. (m)

Is it any wonder then that so many spend money they truly should not be spending or even have? When you spend most of your waking hours at a place you don't like, it is very tempting to feel better by purchasing things. And it works—for a while. When you wear a new outfit, it feels great. However, the feeling goes away quickly. How many of you have stood in front of your closet thinking you have nothing to wear even though there are over 50 outfits in it that YOU bought? If you base your sense of joy on items, you are caught in a vicious cycle of having to buy stuff to bring about a false sense of happiness. Think about it. We live in a country that sells new car fragrance so that we can pretend we are driving a brand new car. The key is to find fulfillment in what you are doing on a daily basis so you aren't compelled to spend money chasing happiness.

Wealthy Life Question

Do you spend money you do not already have? If so, why?

Chapter 2

What Is Debt?

"The rich rules over the poor, and the borrower
is the slave of the lender."

PROVERBS 22:7

It is interesting that Solomon, one of the wealthiest and wisest men to have ever walked Earth, said this, thousands of years ago. This was way before credit cards and department stores. However, the same principle still holds true today. If you owe someone money, you are basically at their mercy. Borrowing money changes the dynamics of any relationship. Debt isn't just a simple financial transaction; in essence, the lender controls the borrower.

Even if you borrow money from a family member, the relationship changes. Let's say you owe your favorite uncle $1,000. You invite him to Thanksgiving dinner but are somewhat ashamed to watch football on your new television set because you know you owe him money and are wondering what he is thinking about this purchase. He may not even be thinking about this but you project it because you feel guilty. Your relationship has changed because of debt. Since this is the case, Solomon is correct: debt does cause a form of slavery in which we are held captive by interest charges, harassing phone calls, or even our own guilt.

What Is Debt?

Many people define debt differently. Some consider debt only what they owe on credit cards and not student loans. Others don't include the money they owe on their house as debt. So what exactly is debt? Debt is any obligation owed by one party—the debtor—to a second party—the creditor. A debt is created when a creditor agrees to lend assets to a debtor. Debt is usually granted with expected repayment and, in most cases, this includes repayment of the original sum along with interest. So, put simply, debt is any money you owe to someone else. This includes your house if you have a mortgage, your car and student loans, and of course credit cards.

Another way we could define debt is spending future income today. When we purchase something we don't have the money for, we are spending our future earnings before we have actually earned them. This means the money we are currently making is already spent. It already has a place to go the second you are paid. And it is not into your bank account!

Debt is the number one obstacle preventing us from living a wealthy life. Think about it. Let's say you feel called to do something but are in debt. It becomes much more difficult to pursue your calling because you owe someone and have to take this into consideration first. Even though most of us know the dangers of accumulating debt, we continue to sign up for more.

Unfortunately, borrowing money has become a way of life for many Americans. The average American drives a car financed by a bank on a road financed by bonds on gas bought with a credit card to the local mall and opens a credit account there to furnish his bank-owned house with things paid for on an installment plan. Take a moment to read this paragraph again. Wow—it is so sad but true!

Credit cards and loans are so common now that many feel it is our Constitutional right to borrow and charge in the pursuit of happiness. After all, more stuff is supposed to lead to a better life. New and better stuff is continuously marketed as evidence of living a prosperous life. Even Thanksgiving, a sacred holiday in which we give thanks for our blessings, has now turned into the kick-off of the accumulation season. We leave our loved ones after stuffing ourselves to go buy them things they will forget about by the time Valentine's Day arrives. To make it even worse, we buy this stuff by borrowing money and, thus, end up further in debt!

The verse at the beginning of this chapter sums it up perfectly: *The rich rules over the poor, and the borrower is the slave of the lender.*

When you have debt you lose some freedom. The deeper you are in debt, the more freedom you lose. When payments drag on for months and even years with the interest eating away at your paychecks, you are unable to live the life you want to because you are repaying debts used for your possessions. You become a slave to the lender.

Most of us get into debt because we are looking to make a quick fix. We are unhappy about something so we buy something to make us feel better. Some call this "retail therapy." While we feel good for a moment, this feeling doesn't last. In fact, we usually feel worse after the high has worn off! We then have to go buy something else, and the cycle begins. Gaining control of debt is far more about your emotions than it is about numbers.

SCARY DEBT STATISTIC

Only 38% of Americans could cover a $1,000 emergency-room visit or a $500 car repair with money they had saved.

The True Cost Of Debt

Many of us accumulate debt on things we really don't need (or for that matter even really want, except for a brief moment in time) without thinking about the future ramifications. Even though paying the minimum payment looks very affordable, you have to understand the true cost of debt.

It is so easy to insert a piece of plastic into a chip reader compared to parting with real dollars. We have an emotional attachment to dollar bills because we know how early we got up and how hard we worked to earn them. Plastic does not make us feel the same way. In fact, we spend 32% more on a vending machine purchase when we use plastic (credit and/or debit card) compared to when we use actual money instead. (a)

Another study shows we spend 12-18% more when using credit cards instead of cash. In addition, McDonald's reports its average ticket is $7 when we use credit cards versus $4.50 when we pay with cash. (b)

There is a reason many of us get numerous credit card offers in the mail each week, and it is not because we are a valued customer. Once you get in debt, it can be a very tough climb out. If someone charges $3,000 on a credit card with an 18% interest rate and just pays the minimum amount each month (2.5%), it will take over 18 years to get rid of this debt! By the time this is paid off, it would have cost almost $7,000: more than double what was originally borrowed!

Some might think, "I use my credit card wisely and pay it off in full each month. In addition, I get points when using my card. Why should I be worried?" Well, it is great that you pay it off every month, but be careful. Sometimes life gets in the way, and if we are careless we could miss a payment. This would lead to late fees plus having to pay interest. In addition, I have never heard a millionaire say, "Man, those credit card points were the keys to my financial success." Unfortunately, many people think they are doing well by making the minimum monthly payment on their credit cards. This can destroy their financial future!

To further illustrate why paying the minimum payment can hurt you in the long run, let's say you have a relatively low credit card balance of $500 with an 18% interest rate. We will say your credit card company sets your minimum monthly payment at $15. Not too bad, you might think. If you divide this $500 by $15 (the monthly payment), you should have this debt paid off in 34 months ($15 x 34 = $510). While that may sound right, you will actually not pay it off in full until paying this amount for 46 months: not 34. How can this be? This is compound interest working against you! If you make this $15 payment for 46 months, when all is said and done, you will have paid $690 ($15 x 46) for your $500 purchase, almost 40% more than the original price! This is with only a $500 debt. Imagine if it was $50,000! This is why it is so tough to get out of debt.

For a moment, let's pretend you become so tired of your credit card debt you decide to just stop paying it. The monthly bills come in and you just throw them in the garbage. What happens then?

First, your creditor will most likely contact you if the payment does not arrive by the due date. They may or may not (depending on past payments) charge a late fee. If you ignore this request, your account will become delinquent. This means it is official: you are behind in paying this debt and your creditor reports it to the credit agency. Then, the credit card company will raise your interest rate to the default rate. If you continue to ignore the monthly bills, the next step is bound to get your attention. Threatening letters will arrive in the mail attempting to get you to respond. You may even start to receive calls from collection agencies when you are trying to enjoy time with your family. If this doesn't make you take notice, you may get sued by the lender. If you continue to keep your head buried in the sand, your creditor might place your account in the charge-off category. At this point, they will not expect to see a dime from you; however, you are still not in the clear. Your creditor will probably sell this debt to another company for a fraction of the amount you owe. This "new" collection agency will begin calling you, asking if you can pay any amount on this debt. They hope they can get anything from you (they made a very small investment on collecting this so even if they get you to pay 10% of the balance they will more than likely have made out well).

I haven't even brought up the most obvious consequence: the damage your credit score will face. A poor credit score will impact the interest rate you are charged on other loans. A spontaneous purchase could haunt you for many years, or even decades!

Non-Financial Effects Of Debt

We just went over some of the way debt impacts your finances. Here are some other ways it impacts you that will not be depicted in your bank account.

A. The Emotional Toll

Mental problems can often be directly related to money troubles. People who have debt are more likely than others to be depressed and even contemplate suicide. (c)

Those who struggle to pay off their debts and loans are more than twice as likely to experience a variety of mental health problems such as depression and severe anxiety. (d)

Debt can make one feel hopeless and lost. These feelings can lead to depression. On the other hand, getting out of debt can give you a sense of accomplishment and help you conquer other goals.

B. The Health Toll

Debt can also have an adverse effect on your health. Debt can lead to high blood pressure and mental health issues. (e)

In addition, debt stress can cause you to have headaches, muscle tension, back pain, and digestive tract issues. (f)

Add stress to the mix and you can see that debt can lead to an extremely unhealthy life.

C. The Relational Toll

Debt can be a huge factor in how happy we are with our spouse. Couples who reported disagreeing about finance once a week were over 30 percent more likely to get divorced than couples who reported disagreeing about finances a few times a month. (g)

In addition, almost 80% of couples who divorce say financial reasons are one of the reasons they ended their marriage. (h)

Arguing about money is the top predictor of divorce. (i)

Despite only having mortgage debt, my life can sometimes be pretty hectic. Adding debt to the mix would definitely make it more stressful. Unfortunately, many couples view their debt issues as too much to overcome and give up on their marriage.

D. The Career Toll

Having debt can greatly impact your career. The stress of dealing with debt can have an impact on how productive you are. In addition, you may have to work extra jobs to pay your debt which leads you to focus less on your full-time job. You could also be offered another job that is more fulfilling but pays less. If you need every dollar you earn to pay on your debt, it will be very difficult to do something more meaningful if it pays less.

Good Debt: Is There Such A Thing?

While I don't consider any debt to be good, there are times when debt is necessary for most of us. We usually borrow money to purchase something we don't have the cash for at that moment. As we just discussed, this will end up costing you more in the long run. Although no debt is good, some can make sense it if it allows you to make a purchase that will pay-off in the long term. This pay-off can either increase your net worth or increase your income.

One example of this type of debt is a mortgage. Most of us don't have enough money sitting around to buy a house outright. This is where a mortgage comes into play. Over a number of years, a house should appreciate in value which will increase your net worth.

Another example of good debt is a student loan. Now, there are many horror stories about the dangers of these loans, but a college degree can lead to many opportunities for some. I am all for graduating college without any debt, but this can be a difficult option for some. This is why a student loan is considered good debt: it is debt that will ultimately pay for itself and help you make more money in the future. You do have to be smart about how much you borrow and what you study so that you can produce enough income to repay the loan. In general, don't accumulate more than one year's salary in student loan debt. Ideally, it will be less than half of your first year's expected pay.

Since I am on the topic of student loan debt, I wanted to share a personal experience of when this debt can be bad. After giving a financial presentation to a large group of new teachers, I had one ask me a depressing question. She said she had a lot of student loan debt and wanted my advice on paying it off. Now, the definition of "a lot" varies so I asked her exactly how much debt her student loans totaled. I was not prepared for her answer. She said $180,000! Yes, you read that correctly. She owed $180,000 and chose a career in which the starting salary is around $35,000. After taxes are taken out, she could apply every cent she earns towards this debt for six years, and it still would not be paid off! I point this out to reinforce how careful you need to be when taking on debt—even necessary debt.

A final example of good debt is money used for purchasing or starting a business. If this business provides a worthwhile product and is managed well, the company should do well and could become a good investment. The main thing to remember is that with all three of these debts (mortgage, student loan, and business) you are acquiring debt so it will enable you to earn more money and/or increase your net worth.

If you borrow money to purchase something, the following criteria should be met:

1. The item should be something that will increase in value or produce an income.
2. The value of the item should be equal to or worth more than the amount borrowed to purchase the item.
3. The amount you borrow should be within your ability to repay without placing a strain on your budget.

For example, consider a home purchase. The family home has historically been an appreciating asset which meets our first criteria. If you purchase a house with a decent down payment and use a shorter 15-year loan, its value will be greater than or close to what you owe on it. With the first two criteria met, we consider the third which is where many people went wrong during the housing crisis in 2007-2010. The house you purchase should not be so expensive that the monthly mortgage payments place a strain on your ability to repay. In addition, you should not have to get special type of financing (subprime, interest only, adjustable-rate mortgage, etc.). If you can meet all the criteria listed above, then the money you borrow can be justified.

While the goal is to have zero debt, it is not always realistic for some of us to start out that way. Just remember to try and eliminate this debt as soon as possible. To help you, I am going to discuss a sure-fire method to do this. It's called the Debt Freedom March, and we'll see that a little later in this book.

The Four Types of Debt

When you think of debt, categorize it into one of these forms: terrible debt, bad debt, better debt, or best debt.

A. Terrible Debt

Terrible debt is the worst debt of all. This type of debt charges extraordinary interest and is extremely punitive. Examples include payday loans, pawn loan, car title loans, and rent-to-own loans. Avoid this type of debt at all costs!

B. Bad Debt

Bad debt charges high interest on items that have no value or rapidly drop in value. Examples include credit card and furniture debt.

We have already discussed how destructive credit card debt can be. What about furniture debt? Many of us see those ads which offer no interest for three years. What can be so bad about that? Let me tell you a little secret about these "deals" that the salesperson doesn't mention. Suppose you purchase furniture to upgrade your living room at a total cost of $5,000. The interest rate is 20%, but because it is interest-free for three years, you won't have to worry about it as you know you will have it paid off by then. You do a great job making the monthly payments, and after 36 months only owe $100 on this loan. You are a little disappointed because it isn't fully paid off but you aren't too upset. You reason that because you only owe $100, at the most you will pay $120 if you add the 20% interest to this amount. I hate to be the bearer of bad news but you are wrong. You will have to pay 20% interest on the original purchase price of $5,000. So you go from owing $120 to owing $1,100! No wonder you see these horrible plans offered all the time.

C. Better Debt

Better debt is debt that charges reasonable interest rates on items that produce a return on investment. This type of debt increases your net worth or income. Take a guess at an example of better debt. Hint: we discussed this earlier in this chapter. If you said mortgage or student loan debt, you win! These two types of debt usually offer relatively low interest rates. Your house should help you increase your net worth over time and a student loan should help you increase your income.

D. Best Debt

If one were to have debt, this is the best type! This debt has reasonable interest charges on items that are passed on to someone or something else. Examples of best debt include rental real estate, commercial real estate and business equipment.

Let's take a look at rental real estate. If you own a home and rent it out to someone else, this person will be paying your mortgage for you! Let's pretend you buy a $120,000 home and put $20,000 down on this. You borrow the remaining $100,000 for 15 years at a 4% interest rate. The monthly payment (excluding taxes and insurance) would be about $740. To help cover the taxes and insurance, you rent it out for $1,000. A family decides to rent it and lives there for 15 years. If your house increased by 1% each year, it would now be worth a little over $139,000. You decide to sell it at this point for that amount. You will have made $119,000 from your $20,000 investment (the down payment). Now you can see why this is the best debt!

Wealthy Life Questions

1. What are some examples of good debt? How about bad debt?

2. What "good" debts do you have?

3. What "bad" debts do you have?

4. List all of your debts below. What group would you label each of them – terrible, bad, good or best?

Debt Name, Balance, Payment, Interest, Classification

Chapter 3

First Things First: The Game of Financial Freedom

*"We choose to go to the moon not because it is easy,
but because it is hard."*

JOHN F. KENNEDY

Before we get started, I want to take a minute and warn you that gaining control of your finances might not be easy. In fact, it could be one of the most difficult things you ever do. However, if life was easy, everyone would have a great marriage, be able to run a marathon, and have millions of dollars in the bank. It is often through those difficult challenges that we grow the most.

While the primary focus of this book is to help you get out of debt, I also want you to take a holistic view of your finances. Such a view often helps you want to attack your debt with much more intensity because you see what it leads to: a wealthy life! You may be enticed to attack your debt like crazy right now, but if you don't understand the steps you must take first, you could end up totally broke again!

A Wealthy Life

So what exactly is a wealthy life? For some it is driving a fancy sports car whereas for others, it can mean living in a huge house. However, I view wealth as something a little deeper. I view a wealthy life as being able to do what you have been called to do no matter the cost or how much you can make by doing it. Does that get you excited? Imagine going to a job that you actually enjoy! Or having enough money to take your family on a dream vacation and paying cash for it. I am not sure what a wealthy life looks like to you, but my goal is to help you eliminate your debt so that you can achieve it.

Managing Money Is Like A Game

Just like games, there are rules when it comes to managing money. Rules such as "spend less than you earn" and "don't buy stuff you cannot afford." If you follow such rules, you will gain traction in your financial life. If you don't follow these rules, you may still do okay financially—but not for long. You see, every action has a consequence. This consequence may not be felt immediately, but it will be felt at some point. This is where winning at the Game of Financial Freedom can help you greatly. It lists the levels you need to conquer in order to start living a wealthy life.

In this book, we are mainly focusing on 7th and 10th levels, but I wanted to give you a look at the entire "game" so you can see why it is so important to get out of debt and what awaits you when you do.

Winning the Game of Financial Freedom

Power-up
(Get Ready to Play!)

Know Your Why/Set Goals

In any area of life we want to have success in, we first must have something we are aiming for. Zig Ziglar said, "Lack of direction, not lack of time, is the problem. We all have 24-hour days." This is so true.

When it comes to your money, having goals is extremely important. Unfortunately, many people let their current financial situation dictate the size of their dreams and goals. Don't let this be you! Set your goals and then work to achieve them, no matter where you stand right now. It might take you awhile to get there, but that is okay.

Goal setting is the first level to pass in The Game of Financial Freedom because it helps you know **WHY** you want to become debt free. In addition to setting goals, we also need to know why we are setting these goals. You see, many of us are just anxious to get out of debt and handle our money better because we are sick and tired of not winning with our finances. While those are good reasons, they do not define your "why." Your "why" will keep you going during those tough stretches and trust me, there will be a few bumps on the road during your Debt Freedom March.

Most people can explain what they do; some can explain how they do it; but very few can clearly articulate why. "Why" is not money or profit; those are results. Your "Why" will propel you to financial success faster than anything else because it is rooted to your core, your calling.

The reason we need to determine our "Why" is that it helps us understand our values and what is truly important to us. For instance, asking, "Why is money important to me?" reveals desires that we don't usually think about. Asking and answering this question can take us out of our comfort zones but recognizing why you want to do better with money is a great first step in aligning your financial decisions with your values.

In the book *Man's Search For Meaning*, Viktor Frankl, a Holocaust survivor, wrote, "When you know your why, you can endure any how." We spend most of our lives focused on the how. This is composed of the obligations and stuff we have to do: basically, life's to-do list. Many times we forget why we are doing these things; we just try to cross them off our endless list of things we need to get done.

I am not saying these things don't need to get done, but when we focus on the why, we look at these a little differently. You are probably going to stumble at some point on your Debt Freedom March. Your "why" will help you persevere and continue on, even though things might be tough.

In addition to knowing our why, we need to know what we are aiming for. Some want to be able to stay home when the kids arrive whereas others want to take great, paid-for-in-advance vacations every year. There is no right or wrong answer; it is personal and based on your own individual hopes and dreams.

One of my financial goals is to have $1 million in investments when I retire. I know many people want to become millionaires, but they don't know why. One of my "why's" in this area is to be able to take special, paid-for-in-cash vacations with my family regardless of the cost. This came to light a few years ago. At that point, I was teaching special needs students. One of my students was too sick to attend school so two afternoons per week, after school dismissed, I would go to his house and teach him. I got paid extra for doing this. I did not count this money as part of our income; I just threw it into a jar and let it accumulate.

After a year, I decided to count it. I had accumulated a good amount and Tracy and I decided to do something special for our girls: we took them to Disney World! This was so much fun, and I loved every minute of it. One of the things I would like to do is be able to take my future grandchildren there every year. In order to do this, we must have minimal debt and a sizable nest egg waiting for us when we retire. This is one of my "whys" for being completely debt free and investing for my future every month. I could come up with a bunch of other ways I could use the money, but because I have a powerful "why," I continue to focus on this instead.

I have heard it said that people lose their way when they

lose their why. Knowing your "why" sets you up for financial success.

Level 1

Get Health, Automobile and Homeowner's/Renter's Insurance

This first level doesn't need too much explanation. Many of us have heard horror stories of those who were not properly insured.

Being properly insured is an important part of your financial plan, perhaps the MOST important part! I know no one likes to pay insurance premiums (myself included). We think of other things we could be doing with that money. I hate to be the bearer of bad news but bad stuff is going to happen! You or a family member will get sick. Your roof will leak. You may have a fender-bender. You can pretend none of these will happen, but that doesn't change anything except that you won't be adequately prepared when one of these events does happen. Insurance protects you when life happens.

What is the purpose of insurance? Insurance eliminates the risk of unpredictable and uncontrollable bills by converting them into a predictable and affordable series of insurance payments. Insurance transfers risk from you to the insurance company. It is as simple as that.

It is important to be properly insured. However, you can also be wasting money and be overly insured. Here are some insurance policies I would recommend you avoid:

Cancer Insurance

Accidental Death Insurance

Mortgage Insurance

Credit Card Insurance

All these policies play on your emotions. What if you die in an accident? How will your spouse pay the bills? That is where your term life insurance comes into play. What if you get cancer? That is where health insurance comes into play. If you really feel the need to purchase these policies, make sure you have the must-need policies in place first.

The importance of having health insurance hit home for me a few years ago. My brother, Kyle, is a very fit and active firefighter. However, it was discovered that he had been born with a hole in his heart, and needed open heart surgery to correct this! I cannot even begin to imagine what his medical bills would have been had he not had health insurance. He turned an unpredictable and uncontrollable bill into a predictable one by paying for health insurance every month.

Like I mentioned above, when we take out insurance, we are transferring risk from us to the insurance provider. For instance, when we take out homeowner's insurance, we pay a fraction of what it would cost to rebuild our house if something were to happen to it. When I lived in Florida, my house was struck by a hurricane. It did some damage and we needed to replace our roof, our back porch, and most of our carpet. Since I had homeowner's insurance, I just paid my premium and the insurance company took care of the rest.

If you are renting, you need to have renter's insurance. Your landlord's policy will not cover your belongings if something were to happen. So, if there were a fire and all was lost, renter's insurance would be the only thing that would replace it.

You can make the proper financial decisions throughout your life and then one slip off a ladder can derail your entire financial future. Many of you already have health, automobile, and homeowner's insurance. In the next two levels we are going to discuss insurance that you may not have now, but need to get as soon as possible.

Level 2

Get Disability Insurance

While it is very important to save money in an emergency fund, get out of debt, and save for retirement, I think obtaining the protection we will talk about in the following three levels is even more important. The first of these is disability insurance.

Think of disability insurance as paycheck insurance. If you became disabled and were no longer able to work, would you be able to pay all of your bills? This is where disability insurance comes into play.

Many workplaces offer both short- and long-term disability insurance (check with your human resources department to see if your place of employment does). Like it sounds, short-term disability insurance would kick in much sooner than long-term disability insurance if you became injured and were unable to work. Both of these types of policies start paying after a set number of days.

The premiums for short-term coverage are more expensive than for long-term, because a short-term policy pays out faster than a long-term one does. My long-term policy would go into effect after 90 days of me being unable to work and will pay me 60 percent of my salary until I am able to collect Social Security. I pay about $20 a month for this coverage. Since we have an emergency fund in place, we could use that for three months if I couldn't work and then start collecting on this policy. If you are just starting out and have nothing saved yet, you might want to consider signing up for a short-term disability policy so you would start getting paid immediately (make sure you check your individual policy to determine if there is a waiting period) rather than having to wait 90 days. However, because this short-term policy costs more, once you have an emergency fund in place that will cover at least 3 months' worth of expenses (90 days), you can sign up for the long-term coverage only and save money each month.

I know we don't plan on becoming injured, but it can happen. What if I was putting up Christmas lights and fell off the ladder and could no longer work? My disability insurance will replace some of my monthly income. In fact, 5.6 percent of working Americans will experience a short-term disability (six months or less) due to illness, injury, or pregnancy, on average every year. (a)

This is an important part of your financial plan and can help keep you out of debt. Check with your benefits department to see how much this will cost you.

Level 3
Get Life Insurance

I know this can be a touchy subject because most of us do not like to think about passing away. I have done a lot of research on this topic (all of about five seconds) and have come up with a great realization. If you are reading this, one day you will die. I don't know when (now that would be scary if I could predict that!) but all we are promised is our last breath.

If you have people who are dependent on your salary to pay the bills, it is important to have life insurance. Life insurance is protection against the loss of income if you pass away and still have financial obligations. Your beneficiary will receive the policy benefit amount. For example, if you had a $100,000 life insurance policy and named your spouse as your beneficiary, he/she would receive that amount if you die.

The goal of life insurance is to provide financial security for your loved ones after you die. Because this is the case, you need to determine your financial situation and how much of your income would need to be replaced if you suddenly passed. For example, do you have young children who need money for college or do you have a lot of debt? If so, you need to have a policy large enough to pay for these expenses. In my case, I have two daughters who might need money for college, along with weddings. I have a life insurance policy that would enable Tracy to pay off our house, not have to work until the girls became adults, and pay for the girls' college and wedding costs if I were to die.

Many financial experts recommend carrying a policy that is ten times your yearly income. The assumption is that your family could invest this money and, if they earned 10 percent a year on it, replace your income. For example, if you make $50,000 a year and had a life insurance policy of $500,000, your family could invest this $500,000 and, if they earned 10 percent per year, replace your yearly income.

Buying a life insurance policy can be somewhat confusing. There are two basic types: term and whole life. Term insurance is like it sounds: it covers for a stated term such as 10 or 20 years. Whole life usually provides both a death benefit (like term) and a cash savings built into it as well.

With term insurance, you don't get anything back if you continue to live, which is a good problem to have. An easy way to think about term insurance is to compare it to renting a house. The beginning payments are less expensive than owning a house but the rent can increase every few years. In addition, if you move, you don't get anything back.

A whole life policy is like buying a house. You lock into a certain rate (like a mortgage) and you know exactly what your payments will be. In addition, you are building savings in a whole life policy. If you cash it in before you pass, you will get some money back (just like if you sell your house, you will get the equity you have in it).

The main benefit of term is the price you pay; it's usually much less expensive than whole life. You may have heard the expression "Buy term insurance and invest the difference." Since a whole life policy costs more, this theory holds that you take the difference between what you are paying for term insurance compared to what you would be paying for whole life and invest this amount.

I have heard the pros and cons of both types of life insurance plans. The most important thing is to make sure you obtain some sort of life insurance to protect your family if they depend on your income to live.

Level 4
Get A Will

I know far too many people who put off getting a will. It does seem very complicated and a big hassle. Even if your only major possession is your house, you still need a will, as it could take years for the courts to figure out who gets it. If you have minor children, you especially need to get one RIGHT NOW! I mean put this book down and do it. A will details exactly where your children will live in case you die. Do you really want to leave that up to some judge?

You also need to keep in mind that wills are state-specific. For instance, when Tracy and I lived in Florida we had a will done there. Upon moving to Georgia, we needed one here to replace the one we had in Florida.

In addition to your will, you also need healthcare power of attorney and a living will. Healthcare power of attorney stipulates the person who will make health decisions for you if you cannot. In addition to obtaining this document, I also think it is a great idea to discuss your wishes with your power of attorney. The living will spells out exactly what you want done if you were in a position that you were alive but could not communicate and needed machines to keep you from passing. When we were in Florida, there was a case in which a woman was in a coma and pretty much nonresponsive. Her husband said her wishes were to be allowed to die but her parents said no. She ended up living in this state for 15 years. (b)

A living will would have spared her loved ones more anguish than they were already facing.

I know these forms might seem expensive but I have some great news for you. You can obtain all the forms for under $150! Dave Ramsey has a bundle that includes a last will and testament, health power of attorney and finance power of attorney. Here is the link: https://www.daveramsey.com/store/product/mama-bear-complete-will-package

I will admit these forms can be a little complicated to complete, but you can do it. I would suggest finding a time when the kids are sleeping and you can concentrate fully on them. You will need to have portions of these notarized, but most banks offer this service.

Before ordering this bundle, I called around to some local attorneys to ask about setting up a basic will and the lowest quote I got to do this was for $250. So even though you will have to spend some time completing this information yourself, you can save a lot of money and leave a lasting legacy to your family and loved ones.

Level 5
Save One Month of Expenses

Having saved money provides margin. What is margin? It is space. Financial margin creates space. I recommend you begin to create this margin by saving one month of expenses. You may not get to this point in one month but start small. Let's say you are able to find a way to save one-fourth of this amount. Do this for four months and, violà, there is your starter emergency fund. This amount will not cover a major emergency but could pay for those minor, unexpected things that happen such as your heat going out or needing new tires on your car. You will eventually add more to this fund but starting by saving one month of expenses is a great step in the right direction.

Don't be concerned with earning interest on this money; it is there to help you avoid paying interest. You should have easy access to this money and be able to get it at a moment's notice. You don't want to have it in a place where you'll be tempted to use it for non-emergencies but you also don't want it to be locked up in a CD where you might have to pay a penalty in order to have access to it. Tracy and I have our emergency fund in a savings account at our local bank. This has worked well for us.

Now I know you are anxious to start tackling debt as soon as possible (this is probably why you are reading this book). In fact, you might even think I am not good at math because it makes no sense, from a mathematical point of view, to put money in a savings account that is paying little interest compared with paying off a high interest credit card. You are correct—sort of. As I established earlier in this book, the math isn't what gets most of us into financial trouble. We need to change our financial behavior, and the way we feel about money, to start winning with it. It can be very tempting to skip a level but think what happens when you do that in real life: you miss out on learning valuable information. Don't skip levels!

Level 6
Invest $100/Month For Retirement

It is important to start investing as soon as possible to take advantage of the magic of compound interest in order to help us achieve some of those goals we listed way back when we were getting ready to play the Game of Financial Freedom.

I think it is extremely important to get out of debt as fast as you can, so saving money for something that could be 40 years away might not make much sense to you. I completely understand that point but let me explain why I think you need to save for retirement as soon as possible, even before tackling your debt.

Many have the best intentions to get out of debt, but for one reason or another, just don't manage to do this. They then get to a point where they want to retire but cannot, because they have nothing saved for these years. In addition, they still have some debt. That is no good! I would like you to start by just investing a small amount into your retirement account: $100 a month. This may sound like a lot to start with but it really is not much of a sacrifice. If you invest this in a 401(k) or 403(b) account this money is invested pre-tax. This means that $100 would only equal a $75-paycheck difference if you are in the 25 percent tax bracket (if you did not invest this $100, it would be taxed before you were paid and, thus, it would equal only $75 more in your check). If you are just starting your career, I want you to do this before you become reliant on your full monthly check. If you have been working a few years, this loss in net income may be a little more noticeable, but it amounts to less than $3 a day!

What can $100/month do for you? Let's say you started investing this amount starting at age 30. You did this for 35 years (until you turned 65) and earned an average of 8% a year on this investment. How much do you think you would have? If you said over $214,000 you are correct! This compound interest thing is pretty powerful.

To show you why it is so important to begin investing as soon as possible, let's take a look at two friends who we will call John and Robert. John got a head start on Robert and began investing $2,000 a year for eight years starting when he was 19 years old. His investments averaged 12 percent growth per year. After eight years, when he was 26 years old, John stopped contributing but his investments still grew at an average rate of 12 percent per year. In all, he invested $16,000.

It took Robert a little bit longer to start investing and he did not begin to do so until he was 27 years old. However, like his friend, Robert contributed $2,000 a year and averaged 12 percent growth on his investments. He did this until he turned 65, so he invested a total of $78,000.

When they both turned 65, John and Robert decided it was time to retire. You may realize this is a trick question but take a guess at who has more in their retirement account: John, who invested a total of $16,000 over eight years, or Robert, who invested a total of $78,000 over 39 years.

Let's take a look:

John Age	Invests	Value plus interest	John Age	Invests	Value plus interest	Robert Age	Invests	Value plus interest	Robert Age	Invests	Value plus interest
19	2000	2240	43	0	189168	19	0		43	2000	109499
20	2000	4749	44	0	211869	20	0		44	2000	124879
21	2000	7558	45	0	237293	21	0		45	2000	142104
22	2000	10706	46	0	265768	22	0		46	2000	161396
23	2000	14230	47	0	297660	23	0		47	2000	183004
24	2000	18178	48	0	333379	24	0		48	2000	207204
25	2000	22599	49	0	373385	25	0		49	2000	234308
26	2000	27551	50	0	418191	26	0		50	2000	264665
27	0	30857	51	0	468374	27	2000	2240	51	2000	298665
28	0	34560	52	0	524579	28	2000	4749	52	2000	336745
29	0	38708	53	0	587528	29	2000	7558	53	2000	379394
30	0	43352	54	0	658032	30	2000	10706	54	2000	427161
31	0	48554	55	0	736995	31	2000	14230	55	2000	480660
32	0	54381	56	0	825435	32	2000	18178	56	2000	540579
33	0	60907	57	0	924487	33	2000	22599	57	2000	607688
34	0	68216	58	0	1035425	34	2000	27551	58	2000	682851
35	0	76802	59	0	1159676	35	2000	33097	59	2000	767033
36	0	85570	60	0	1298837	36	2000	39309	60	2000	861317
37	0	95383	61	0	1454698	37	2000	46266	61	2000	966915
38	0	107339	62	0	1629261	38	2000	54058	62	2000	1085185
39	0	120220	63	0	1824773	39	2000	62785	63	2000	1217647
40	0	134646	64	0	2043746	40	2000	72559	64	2000	1366005
41	0	150804	65	0	2288996	41	2000	83506	65	2000	1532166
42	0	168900				42	2000	95767			

As hard as it may be to believe, John's investment would outgrow Robert's by more than $700,000! As you can see, John would have $2,288,996 and Robert would have $1,532,166. How does this happen? Starting to invest as early as possible is the key. His $16,000 invested turns into almost $2.3 million. THAT is the power of compound interest!

With many companies doing away with the traditional pension, it is now common they offer some sort of matching retirement plan. If your employer offers a company match, please take advantage of that. Even though a company match is a huge benefit, only 77 percent of employees who participate in an employer-sponsored retirement plan contribute enough to receive the full employer match. For employees earning less than $35,000 a year, only 64 percent receive the full match. (c)

These individuals are missing out on a great gift: FREE MONEY! To illustrate this more clearly, we will say Tom works for a company that matches up to 3 percent of the contributions he makes into his 401(k). Tom makes $48,000 a year which would be $4,000/month. Three percent of $4,000 is $120. So, Tom would invest $120 each month. The company matches this amount so the total Tom would be investing is $240/month. Here is where it gets even better. Tom is in the 25 percent income tax bracket. This means his paycheck would be only $90 less each month, because money invested in a 401(k) is done before taxes are taken out. If Tom did not invest this $120, he would only see $90 more in his paycheck (25 percent of $120 equals $30; $120 minus $30 equals $90). So, Tom would be investing $240 (his $120 contribution along with the $120 company match) a month and only miss $90 to do this! Even if Tom earned 0 percent on his investments, he will be making money. In one year, he would have invested $1,080 ($90 per each of 12 months) but would have $2,880 in his retirement account! If Tom did this for 30 years, he would have invested a total of $32,400 and have $86,400 in his account. This is assuming he earned nothing on his investments! What if Tom's investments averaged 10 percent growth over these 30 years? He will have over $495,000 in his account! That's right—over ten times the amount he invested. All this for $3 a day. For the price of a Diet Coke from a vending machine a day, Tom could have almost half a million dollars in his retirement account. This is why you need to take advantage of a company match if you are ever offered one. Your company will be helping you retire!

If your place of employment does not offer a retirement plan, open your own account and start contributing at least $100 a month. This is important because we want to take advantage of the power of compound interest for as many years as possible.

Level 7

Eliminate All Debt Except The Mortgage

Finally, in the seventh level, we focus on getting out of debt. In The Game of Financial Freedom, 7th level is the when we conquer something we've been playing with for a long time: DEBT!

Some of the common types of debt we focus on here include credit card balances, car loans, student loans, furniture, and debts owed to family and friends.

This requires some discipline and determination but the pay-off is well worth it. When you can keep more of your hard-earned money instead of paying someone else, you will find you can live on a lot less. In addition, when you use the money you have been paying someone else and instead pay this same money to yourself, you can build up a huge margin and begin to see how those goals you set when powering-up to play can become a reality.

During financial presentations when I'm teaching these steps, people sometimes ask, "Doesn't it make more sense to pay off debt before starting an emergency fund?" The answer is absolutely! From a mathematical standpoint, it makes much more sense to pay off a debt with a 24 percent interest rate than it does earning 1 percent on your money in a savings account. However, if we are in debt, we have to remember that the math probably didn't get us there. Most of us know it's not wise to buy things on credit but did so anyway.

Let's take a look at the outcome if you pay off your debt first rather than saving anything in an emergency fund. You are plugging along and doing a great job; in fact, you have already paid off two credit cards. One cold winter morning you go to start your car and the battery is dead. You don't have any money so how in the world are you going to pay for this? Yep, you guessed it, back on the credit card it goes. Many people already feel they can't handle money and here is yet another blow to their self-esteem. At this point, a lot of us might throw in the towel and revert back to our old spending habits. It can be very tempting to skip a level, but don't! Each level of the Game of Financial Freedom teaches you important lessons to help you achieve financial success.

SCARY DEBT STATISTIC

Two reports published in 2015 by the Pew Charitable Trusts found that 55% of households didn't have enough liquid savings to replace a month's worth of lost income and that of the 56% of people who said they'd worried about their finances in the previous year, 71% were concerned about having enough money to cover everyday expenses.

Level 8

Save At Least Three Months of Expenses

I realize that three months of expenses may sound like a huge number but let's take a look and see how quickly this can be accomplished. Let's say you needed $3,000/month to live before advancing to this level. You already saved up one month of expenses in Level 5. You might think you now need to save $6,000 more to have a total of three months of expenses saved. Hold up! Suppose you have been paying $500/month towards your debt while you were in Level 7. Once this debt is gone, this money is no longer an expense. In fact, you just reduced your living expenses by $500 a month! Now you just need $2,500 a month to pay for all of your expenses. To cover three months of expenses, you will only need to save $7,500. You already have $3,000 saved so you need to save $4,500 more to have three months of expenses saved. You can now pay yourself the $500 monthly amount that used to go towards your debt. If you do this for nine months, you will have three months of expenses saved!

While the goal in Level 8 is to save at least three months of expenses, I did include the words "at least." Should you aim for more than three months of expenses saved? That is somewhat of a personal question, but I have never talked to someone who said, "Man, I wish I didn't have so much in my savings account." Why would you want to save more? Even though I feel pretty secure in my teaching job, the county I was teaching in had some budget cuts a few years back. In fact, we had 10 unpaid furlough days and some teachers were actually let go. This was a sad situation for them and I would feel devastated if this happened to me. It would be much worse if I did not have anything saved for a situation like this. Having margin in place will enable you to sleep peacefully at night. If the unimaginable happened and you lost your job, you would know that you will continue to have a roof over your head, food to eat, and be able to live life for a period of time without having to work. This will also enable you to take some time and catch your breath. Losing a job is a big life event. You will have some time to process this and then look for another job that you actually would want to have and not just rush into the first thing you see advertised.

Remember, you also want this money to be sufficiently accessible. In addition, this money is meant to be used for emergencies and not to earn a lot of interest. We can be a little more aggressive with the money we invest for our retirement which just happens to be included in the next level.

Level 9
Invest 15 Percent of Your Salary for Long-Term Dreams

With at least three months of savings in place and no debt except the mortgage, you can begin investing 15 percent of your salary to achieve some of those beginning goals you set.

You already started investing $100 a month when you were on Level 6. You are going to increase it now to represent 15 percent of your gross income. The beauty is that you can use the money you freed up in Level 7 to do so. Investments can include mutual funds, stocks, real estate, or perhaps even starting your own business.

Level 10
Pay Off Your Mortgage

The mortgage is the other debt we will discuss in more detail later on. If you are just starting the game, getting to the 10th level can seem pretty daunting. The great thing is that it may not even take you ten years to make it here! When you are at this point, the only debt you will have is your house. Since this is the case, it can be paid off pretty quickly.

Level 11

Invest 30 percent of Your Salary for Long-Term Dreams

Think about this for a minute: if you have no debt at all, including your house, wouldn't it be pretty easy to invest 30 percent of your income? We spend so much of our earnings paying other people. Once we eliminate all our debt, we can easily invest 30 percent and still have plenty left over to live generously, fund our dreams, and do whatever we want!

When we make it to 11th level, part of this 30 percent can be saving for your child's college fund. Notice, I list saving for your child's college in Level 11 and not at the beginning! If you are a parent, you are used to putting your child(ren)'s needs before your own. It is so important to take care of your own financial situation before trying to help your kid(s).

Let's say you decided to invest for your children's college before investing for your retirement. In fact you did so well, they are able to attend elite Ivy League schools. You are able to cover all of their college expenses in full and they graduate and get great jobs. They then marry and begin having children of their own. You are now getting older and ready to retire but cannot because you haven't saved enough. One day your boss announces there will be some severe budget cuts and you are let go.

What will you do now? Unfortunately, many parents get into this situation and have to move in with their children. I am sure Ava and Ella both love me dearly, but I don't want to put them in such a situation. It is my goal to be able to pay for their college, but I am not sacrificing my retirement to do so. They could do well in high school and earn a scholarship. They might have to work during college or not live in the best dorm. At the very worst, they may have to get a student loan. I don't want them to have to get a loan but at least they have that option; the last time I checked, there is no option for a retirement loan.

Think about it: there is a 100 percent chance you will retire one day unless you die before this time. However, there is only a 69 percent chance that your children will go to college. (d) I know that many of us think our kids will go to college (as a family of teachers, Tracy and I feel this way) but the statistics do not lie. Many of us, as parents, feel it is OUR responsibility to pay for all of our child(ren)'s college expenses. In fact, kids feel this way, too! Sixty-two percent of kids 8 to 14 years old expect their parents to cover the cost of "whatever college I want to go to." (e)

Don't fall for this line of thinking. Remember, your retirement should always come before saving for your child's education.

Speaking of college, planning for it can be confusing, given all the options available. You can save for college by investing in ESAs (Educational Savings Accounts), 529s, and even Roth IRAs. I highly recommend you talk this over with your financial advisor so that you can choose the best option for your child(ren).

When planning for college, think about the value you're getting for your money. As a schoolteacher, I would make the same amount whether I have a degree from Yale or from the University of Georgia. According to the College Board, a "moderate" college budget for an in-state public college for the 2019-2020 academic year averaged $26,590 and one at a private college averaged $53,980. These amounts took into account tuition, fees, housing, meals, books, supplies, and personal and travel expenses. (f)

With two daughters who will be graduating from high school in the next six years, I am thinking like many of you: WOWSERS! This is why it is so important to really think long and hard about college. We can no longer send our kids away and give them time to discover themselves. It is way too expensive for that.

I attended a community college for two years, then graduated with my bachelor's degree from a state university and no one has ever held this against me. There are degrees from some universities that mean more than from others but, in many careers, a degree is a degree no matter where one attended.

If you are not able to set enough aside to pay for your child's entire post-secondary education and he has to resort to student loans to help with this, please advise your teen how these loans work.

Many college students do not work, so they borrow enough to pay for their living expenses as well as tuition and other student fees. I encourage you to explain to her that she will have to start paying towards this loan once she graduates, when she is just starting out in life and will have many other expenses to worry about. If your child does need to obtain a student loan, my advice is that she uses it for educational expenses only and gets a job to pay for her living expenses.

In fact, student loan debt is now something that could have severe consequences for our economy. Nearly 50 percent of young Americans begin their working lives with student debt and 43 million Americans have student loans! The total amount of outstanding student loan debt is $1.3 trillion. This comes at a time when the job market is not as strong as in years past.

Student loan debt could force many younger adults to delay important milestones many of us reach, such as getting married, buying a house, and having children. This leads to a slowdown in the housing market, which can affect many of us. Getting a college degree can be very important. Despite this, if you are unable to fund your child's post-secondary education, help her be smart about college debt or she will find herself in the same spot many are in today.

Level 12

Do Whatever You Want and Live a Prosperous Life

Okay, let's take a moment to pause and dream big right now. Think how nice it will be to win the Game of Financial Freedom! You are now in the position to do almost anything you want. Let's say you go to work one Monday morning, and you have just had enough. You know in your heart it isn't what you are meant to do. Guess what? You are in a position to do whatever you want! Since you don't have any debt, you are now in the position where you can look for something else to do, even if it doesn't pay as much as your current job. You can also save up fast and take that dream vacation you have always wanted to go on. The options for having fun are almost unlimited.

You can also continue to have your money grow. You will have a lot more now to invest. You can also save enough money every month to purchase a second house outright and then rent it out. This would bring in income every single month and build your net worth.

However, the greatest thing you will be able to do is bless others. I am not a big fan of others telling me I have to give them some of my hard-earned money, but it feels much differently when you are able to willingly give. Picture yourself stopping at a restaurant and your server is a single mom working to support her family. Think about how cool it would be to leave her a $100 tip! Think of how many families you could bless at Christmas. The list of ways you can truly leave a legacy is endless.

In my life, I am eternally grateful to my Great-Great Uncle Jimmy and my grandmother, who we called Meno. When Uncle Jimmy passed away in the early 90s, he left Meno a relatively small sum of money. Since she was investing already and had money saved for retirement, she could have spent this inheritance on whatever she wanted. Instead of blowing this money, Meno used it to help pay for some of my college expenses. She also used some of it to help my brother, Kyle, attend fire school and become a firefighter. Thanks to these unselfish acts, I was able to become a teacher and have had an impact on hundreds of children and (because of my books) adults, too. Kyle was able to become a fireman and paramedic and save countless lives. In fact, Kyle was even appointed Battalion Chief at the young age of 37. I know Meno and Uncle Jimmy are both smiling down on us, knowing they are still making this world a better place.

Let's Get Out Of Debt

We are about to get into the way for you to eliminate your debt. I want you to make sure you follow the rules of The Game of Financial Freedom, though. I know you are so ready to start paying off your creditors, but by positioning yourself for a successful transition through The Game of Financial Freedom, your Debt Freedom March will be off to a great start.

Wealthy Life Questions

1. What level in The Game of Financial Freedom are you in?

The Game of Financial Freedom

Power-up	Know Your Why/Set Goals
LEVEL 1	Get Health, Auto, and Homeowner's Insurance
LEVEL 2	Get Disability Insurance
LEVEL 3	Get Life Insurance
LEVEL 4	Get a Will
LEVEL 5	Save One Month of Expenses
LEVEL 6	Invest $100/Month for Retirement
LEVEL 7	Eliminate All Debt Except the Mortgage

LEVEL 8	Save at Least Three Months of Expenses
LEVEL 9	Invest 15 percent of Your Salary
LEVEL 10	Pay off Your Mortgage
LEVEL 11	Invest 30 percent of Your Salary
LEVEL 12	Do Whatever You Want/Live a Prosperous Life

2. Have you skipped any levels?

3. For the levels you have not reached yet, set a goal date of when you would like to achieve them!

Chapter 4

Let's Talk About Debt

"We tend to focus on assets and forget about debts. Financial security requires facing up to the big picture: assets minus debts."

SUZE ORMAN

Before we get into tackling your current debt, we must briefly talk about why it is so important to avoid new debt.

As we discussed before, most financial problems don't really have much to do with math. The biggest obstacle when getting out of debt has more to do with behavior than anything else. When in debt, many people feel disappointed in themselves and can't believe they allowed themselves to get into such a situation. This is why it is so important to not take on any new debt when eliminating existing debt; if you do, oftentimes you will feel like a failure (even though you are not) and give up altogether. You may even feel like a hamster running in a wheel. You are running as fast and hard as you can, but are not going anywhere.

This is the reason we reviewed The Game of Financial Freedom levels before we get started on our Debt Freedom March. Life is bound to happen. In fact, I almost guarantee something out of the ordinary will happen just as you are starting or are beginning to make progress. Murphy's Law has a bad habit of showing up at the most inopportune times. This is why we proceed through the Game of Financial Freedom one level at a time.

Following the rules of The Game of Financial Freedom ensures you will have margin in place to help you avoid new debt. When something unexpected happens, you will be able to pay cash to take care of it. The cost of things such as a leaky roof or a minor car repair can be paid without taking on more debt. Sounds like a no-brainer but, one of the keys to eliminating debt is to avoid taking on more debt.

SCARY DEBT STATISTIC

A study by Annamaria Lusardi, Peter Tufano and Daniel Schneider asked individuals whether they could "come up with" $2,000 within 30 days for an unanticipated expense. Slightly more than one-quarter could not and another 19% could do so only if they pawned possessions or took out payday loans. The conclusion: nearly half of American adults are "financially fragile" and "living very close to the financial edge."

Credit Scores

Many of us read and hear about the importance of having a good credit score. Your credit score is basically the simplified version of your credit history rolled up into one three-digit number.

There are five factors that make up your credit score:

Payment history – 35%

Amounts owed – 30%

Length of credit history – 15%

New credit – 10%

Credit type – 10%

So, as you can see, your credit score is really your debt score! It is pretty easy to understand why payment history is the number one factor when determining your credit score, but 30% of it is based on something many don't pay much attention to: the amount you owe. In fact, if you owe too much, this can negatively affect your score.

There is no ideal credit utilization (credit-to-debt) ratio but you should aim to utilize no more than 30% of the credit that is available to you on a card; a lower ratio is better for your score. For instance, if you have a card with a $2,500 credit limit, you do not want to charge more than $750 (30% of $2,500) each month. Even if you pay the balance off in full each month, your credit score will still go down.

While I do not pay a lot of attention to credit scores, having a higher credit score can make your life easier and less expensive. Employers, insurance agents, lenders, and others use your credit score to determine how responsible you are. To lenders, your credit score determines your ability and responsibility in repaying a loan. Your boss may even run a credit check on you to see if you are a responsible employee!

Having bad credit can hinder your ability to purchase a home, or get a certain job, and will cost you money, as you will be charged higher interest rates and fees.

The Three Major Credit Agencies

There are three major credit agencies that give your credit score to people/organizations that want it. These agencies are Equifax, Experian, and Transunion. Each of these agencies collects information about your credit history from sources such as lenders and employers. They then rate your performance to come up with your credit score. Each of these agencies may access different information and has its own formula in determining your score. Since this is the case, your credit score may vary amongst each of them.

I encourage all of you to visit www.AnnualCreditReport.com and complete the information needed to see your credit score and report from each agency. I recently did this myself and it took less than 15 minutes to complete. This is important to do before beginning your Debt Freedom March for several reasons. First, you may have forgotten about a debt that still has a balance. When starting your Debt Freedom March, you will first need to compile a list of all your debts. Obtaining your credit report will enable you to see a clear picture of all your debts. In addition, you might have something on your credit report that is incorrect. You could have paid something off years ago but it was not properly reported. You can now get this removed from your report and, thus, improve your credit score right off the bat.

Understanding Your Credit Score

After completing the information required on AnnualCreditReport.com, you will be given your three-digit credit score from all three agencies. What exactly do these mean? Here is a brief explanation:

800 and Above = Excellent Credit

If your credit score is 800 or above, you have a long credit history and made your payments on time. You have handled all of your debt very well. In addition to having multiple lines of credit, you have had other types as well (mortgage, car loans, etc.). You most likely have a stable work history and don't jump around a lot. You should have no trouble obtaining a loan and will be offered the best interest rates and lowest fees available. If this were school, you would be an A+ student.

Between 750 and 799 = Very Good Credit

If you have a credit score between 750 and 800, you are viewed in the same fashion as those with excellent credit. You may have a higher debt-to-income ratio. This compares the amount you make to the amount you owe. You are still in good standing here and should get many of the same perks as those with excellent credit do.

Between 700 and 749 = Good Credit

If you have good credit, you have a decent credit history and most of your accounts are in good standing. You may have made a late payment along the way which has dropped your score some. Lenders will offer you decent interest rates but not as favorable as those with better credit scores. In addition, your insurance premiums will probably be a bit higher than those with excellent and very good credit.

Between 650 and 699 = Fair Credit

If you are in this category, you have had a few bumps in the past. This could be late payments and/or accounts turned over to a collection agency. In addition, you may just have too much debt. No matter the reason, the lender views you as someone who has a somewhat high risk of defaulting on a loan and, thus, you will probably be required to secure the loan with some sort of collateral.

Between 600 and 649 = Bad Credit

Having bad credit is no fun. You have had credit issues in the past and possibly a few accounts turned over to a collection agency. In addition, you may have even filed for bankruptcy. Unfortunately, it is going to be very difficult to get a loan without having to put down a large down payment or collateral. In addition, you will have higher insurance costs, too. Some employers, especially those in the finance and defense industries, will not hire you if you do not have solid credit. They might believe you pose a risk of employee theft or fraud, or can be enticed to sell information for cash.

Below 599 = Very Bad Credit

This is as bad as it gets. You are more than likely delinquent on multiple accounts and probably have had something repossessed and/or filed for bankruptcy. If you have credit cards, they are either maxed out or closed because of nonpayment. Having very bad credit will negatively impact most of your life. Lenders (except those who specifically focus on people with bad credit) will not approve you for any loan even if you can provide a lot of collateral. Insurance agencies will likely turn you away because you pose a lot of risk. To make matters even worse, employers that check credit will not hire you.

Like I mentioned, I do not want you to focus too much on your credit score and what it is at this point. Even if your score is not good right now, the beauty is that we are going to change that status. Once you get on your Debt Freedom March and take control of your finances, your score will begin to increase.

Prioritize Your Current Debts

In the following chapters we are going to go over how to ditch your debt, create financial margin, pay off your house and speed up your Debt Freedom March. Before getting to these, I want to address another topic: which debts to focus on if you are struggling mightily with your finances.

I know some of you might be facing tough decisions about who will be paid and who will not be paid. At this point in your life, there is just not enough money to pay everyone you owe. If you find yourself in a situation where the financial sky is falling and the walls are closing in on you, it is imperative that you prioritize your spending. The following list is my suggested order of who gets paid when your paycheck runs out before the end of the month.

Housing

You must take care of your mortgage/rent and utilities first. One of our basic needs is shelter so you need a place to live. If you are living in a house that is too costly (the monthly payments exceed more than 30% of your income) it is time to look for a more affordable place to live.

Food

Here is another one of our basic human needs. We have to eat in order to stay alive! Don't get me wrong, I am not talking about fast food or dining at a restaurant here. In fact, if you are in this situation, the only time you should be in a restaurant is if you are working there. Food should be bought using as many coupons as possible with great attention paid to cost. I am all for eating healthy, but when money is tight we are looking for the best deals possible.

Transportation

If you need transportation to earn an income, this is a necessity. If you live somewhere that has public transportation, I suggest using that. You could also carpool or ride a bike to work, depending on where you live.

Back Taxes

The government will do all they can to get the money that is owed to them. They can even legally take money directly out of your paycheck! Remember, there are only two things guaranteed in life: death and taxes.

Secured Debts

Secured debts are ones in which the lender can come and take something. The lender protects itself by making the borrower have some sort of collateral against the loan. For instance, a car payment is a secured debt. The lender can come and take the car if you stop paying on it. Other types of secured debts include boats, motorcycles, and recreational vehicles.

Friends and Family Debts

If you have taken care of the above-mentioned debts and still have money left, now is the time to pay any debts you owe to friends and family. Money issues have destroyed thousands of friendships and wrecked even more families. Don't let this happen to you!

Unsecured Debts

While many people put this type of debt first, money owed on credit cards, student loans, and signature loans should come last! Many of you have heard the old adage, "The squeaky wheel gets the grease." This is why we focus on these types of debts and neglect the other debts. Unsecured debt holders are the ones who holler the loudest to get your attention. They know they cannot take anything from you so they bark the loudest and play on your emotions to get you to pay them first. The sad thing is it works. There are some who pay their credit cards and not their mortgage. This is not good!

If you find yourself in this situation, review your spending plan to make sure your priorities are in order.

Be Content With What You Have

Before we take a look at ways to get out of debt, we need to keep this mentality in mind. I realize feeling content and happy with what we have is totally based on our current perspective, but sometimes we need to step outside our small boxes and the current situation in our lives to realize how blessed we truly are.

Before we get into the strategies for paying off your debt, take some time and make a list, in the spaces below, of everything for which you are grateful:

I'm grateful for ....

1.
2.
3.
4.
5.
6.
7.
8.
9.
10.
11.
12.
13.
14.
15.
16.
17.
18.
19.
20.

I also encourage you to challenge each member of your family to list the things they are grateful for, too.

For some of you, there is not enough room to list everything you are grateful for, whereas for others, you might not be able to think of more than ten right now. That is okay. Just refer back to this page often (I encourage you to do so at least one time every day for at least one month) and I bet many ideas will come pouring in.

An Attitude of Gratitude

I know it can be easy to get caught up in all the things we need to accomplish in a day, but something that really helps me is my morning routine. I am usually up around 4:00, so that I can work out before I head off to school. Before heading to the gym, I spend time with God and read the Bible. I reflect on all my blessings. I am a Christian, but even if you are not, you can still spend some time reflecting on the positive things you have in your life. It may not seem like much, but even having the ability to read these words is a blessing.

Something else that has changed the way I look at life is teaching special needs children. I teach what is known in Georgia as a self-contained Profound Class. The students in my class have profound mental and physical disabilities and their IQs are under 30. All of my students are in wheelchairs, some have to be tube-fed, all need assistance with toileting and have communication needs. However, despite these limitations, most of them are extremely happy. I feel pretty silly complaining about my situation when I am able to do much more than they are. Some have said that these students are lucky to have me as their teacher, but I know the opposite is true. I am the lucky one, and the lessons they teach me will last a lifetime!

Wealthy Life Question

How can you avoid taking on any new debt?

Chapter 5

Debt Freedom March

"Too many people spend money they haven't earned, to buy things they don't want, to impress people they don't like."
WILL ROGERS

Let The Fun Begin

It is now time to eliminate your debt! Earlier we talked briefly about the power of compound interest and how $100/month could turn into more than $200,000 over time. Even one of the smartest men to ever walk earth had something to say about compound interest. Albert Einstein said, "The most powerful force in the universe is the power of compound interest." If someone as wise as Einstein observed this, I definitely want it working for me!

SCARY DEBT STATISTIC

In a survey of American finances published in 2015 by Pew, 60% of respondents said they had suffered some sort of "economic shock" in the past 12 months: a drop in income, a hospital visit, the loss of a spouse, a major repair. More than half struggled to make ends meet after their most expensive economic emergency. Even 34% of the respondents who made more than $100,000 a year said they felt strain as a result of an economic shock.

When you are paying interest, you are doing the complete opposite. You are going against the most powerful force in the financial universe. This is why it is so important to eliminate your debt in order to win with your money.

Document Your Debt Reality

Where do we begin? First, we need to calculate how long it will take us to become debt free. We start by listing every non-house and non-business debt we owe. You need to know the following: the name of the debt, how much you currently owe, and the minimum monthly payment. To help illustrate this, we are going to pretend you have the following debts:

NAME OF DEBT	BALANCE YOU OWE	MONTHLY PAYMENT
Credit Card	$5000	$100
Student Loan	$10,000	$250
Car Loan	$12,500	$300
Total Debt	$27,500	$650

Because you know the importance of not accumulating any new debt (and therefore, won't add to the total), we are going to use just these debts when calculating how long it will take you to eliminate it. We will view these three obligations as one big debt totaling $27,500. We will also add up the total monthly payments on these debts to pretend you are making one big payment. This equals $650. Next, we divide the total debt owed ($27,500) by the overall monthly payments ($650) and we will be debt free in 42.3 months. Now, I know at this point some of you might be asking, "What about the interest?" This a great question because we did not include this in our calculation. There is a reason for this omission. Interest charges will definitely have an impact on eliminating debt. However, many times when people attack their debt with focus and intensity, they actually eliminate it within the calculated time frame and, in some cases, even sooner! In an upcoming chapter, we are going to go over some ways you can speed up this process for you, too!

Eliminate Your Debt

There are two basic debt reduction strategies offered by most financial coaches. One strategy is to focus on debts with the highest interest rates first and eliminate these as quickly as possible. While this makes great mathematical sense, we have to remember that math did not get us into debt. Our financial behavior led to it. The difficult part about this method is the follow through. You see, you might have a high interest debt of $20,000 with a payment of $250/month. It would take you over six years to pay this off! While this is possible, six years is a long time to focus on one debt. Many of us would grow tired, and with one little financial challenge, we would give up. We may just figure we will have a credit card payment forever and not stay fired up about paying it off. This is where the other method comes into play: The Debt Snowball. It is my preferred method.

The Debt Snowball

In the debt snowball method, you focus on the smallest debt first and proceed from there. You list debts in order from least to greatest balance owed and just move down the list; remember, we are not focusing on the interest rates with this method, but the balance owed. This works well because of the emotional and noticeable impact. Once you pay off that first debt, you get a morale boost and are motivated to keep going. When you no longer have to write a check for one of the debts, you immediately notice you are making progress! Then you focus on paying off the next debt and the momentum is really rolling now. This is very similar to being on a diet. If you lose two pounds the first week, you realize your hard work and effort are worth it and are motivated to lose even more. Once you get the snowball rolling, it can quickly become an avalanche.

Here are the steps you can take to apply the Debt Snowball to your debt:

1. Restructure high interest debt to lower interest rates.
2. List your debts from the smallest amount owed to the largest.
3. Pay minimum payments on all debts - except the smallest amount owed.
4. Apply all additional money to the smallest debt.
5. When the smallest debt is eliminated, take the monthly payment you were paying for that debt and add it to the monthly payment you are making on the smallest remaining debt.
6. Continue this process with intense focus until you are DEBT FREE!

The Debt Snowball In Action

To see how great this is, we need to see how this works in the real world with real numbers. We are not going to list our mortgage debt at this point; that comes later when we are in Level 10. We are going to list all other debt. So let's say you have the following debts:

Credit Card 1 $5,100
Credit Card 2 $2,900
Car 1 $15,200
Car 2 $12,250
Student Loan $16,250
Doctor $1,000

Now we are going to put them in order from least to greatest and list what we pay on each of these debts every month.

Debt Name	Balance	Monthly Payment
Doctor	$1,000	$100
Credit Card 2	$2,900	$100
Credit Card 1	$5,100	$150
Car 2	$12,250	$400
Car 1	$15,200	$500
Student Loan	$16,250	$200
Total Debt	$52,700	$1,450

In this example, you have a total of $52,700 in debt and pay $1,450 towards this every month. Once again we are not calculating the interest, just the actual debt amount owed. If we divide $52,700 by $1,450, you would eliminate this debt in 36.3 months, a little over three years.

Let's see how we can speed that up a bit. Remember, we are going to make minimum payments on all our debts except the one we owe the least amount on. Suppose we free up an extra $100 a month to apply to our smallest debt (only about $3 a day!). This is what our DFD calculation looks like now:

Debt Name	Balance	Monthly Payment
Doctor	$1,000	$200
Credit Card 2	$2,900	$100
Credit Card 1	$5,100	$150
Car 2	$12,250	$400
Car 1	$15,200	$500
Student Loan	$16,250	$200
Total Debt	$52,700	$1,550

DFD: 34 months (two years, 10 months)

Because we are tackling the smallest debt first, we apply this extra $100 to the Doctor and continue paying the same as what we have been on the rest of our debts. After five months, the doctor debt will be gone! So this is what our debt picture would look like:

Debt Name	Balance	Monthly Payment
Doctor	PAID OFF!	(Freed Up $200)
Credit Card 2	$2,400	$100
Credit Card 1	$4,350	$150
Car 2	$10,250	$400
Car 1	$12,700	$500
Student Loan	$15,250	$200

Now that we no longer owe the Doctor, we have freed up another $200/month. We are going to continue using the snowball and apply this $200 to the next smallest debt – in this case Credit Card 2. We have been paying $100/month on this debt so we will now pay $300/month. Here is how our debts look now:

Debt Name	Balance	Monthly Payment
Doctor	PAID OFF!	(Freed Up $200)
Credit Card 2	$2,400	$300
Credit Card 1	$4,350	$150
Car 2	$10,250	$400
Car 1	$12,700	$500
Student Loan	$15,250	$200
Total Debt	$44,950	$1,550

DFD: 29 months (2 years, 5 months)

If we did this for eight months, one of our credit cards will be paid-off! Here is what our debt picture looks like now:

Debt Name	Balance	Monthly Payment
Doctor	PAID OFF!	(Freed Up $200)
Credit Card 2	PAID OFF!	(Freed Up $100)
Credit Card 1	$3,150	$150
Car 2	$7,050	$400
Car 1	$8,700	$500
Student Loan	$13,650	$200
Total Debt	$32,550	$1,550

So what is your next step? You guessed it: we add the $300 we have been paying on Credit Card 2 to what we are paying on the other credit card. Here is what that looks like:

Debt Name	Balance	Monthly Payment
Doctor	PAID OFF!	(Freed Up $200)
Credit Card 2	PAID OFF!	(Freed Up $100)
Credit Card 1	$3,150	$450
Car 2	$7,050	$400
Car 1	$8,700	$500
Student Loan	$13,650	$200
Total Debt	$32,550	$1,550

DFD: 21 months (1 year, 9 months)

Well, seven months later, Credit Card 1 is paid off! How great would this feel? In less than two years, you will have paid off three debts with two of those being credit cards! Here is your updated debt picture:

Debt Name	Balance	Monthly Payment
Doctor	PAID OFF!	(Freed Up $200)
Credit Card 2	PAID OFF!	(Freed Up $100)
Credit Card 1	PAID OFF!	(Freed Up $150)
Car 2	$4,250	$400
Car 1	$5,200	$500
Student Loan	$12,250	$200
Total Debt	$21,700	$1,550

Now we can see how this snowball really starts growing! You are going to take the $450 you have been paying on Credit Card 1 and apply it to the next debt: Car 2. So here is what your overall debt picture will now look like:

Debt Name	Balance	Monthly Payment
Doctor	PAID OFF!	(Freed Up $200)
Credit Card 2	PAID OFF!	(Freed Up $100)
Credit Card 1	PAID OFF!	(Freed Up $150)
Car 2	$4,250	$850
Car 1	$5,200	$500
Student Loan	$12,250	$200
Total Debt	$21,700	$1,550

DFD: 14 months

Do this for five months and BAM!—one of the car payments is gone! See how quickly this happens? Now your debt picture looks like this:

Debt Name	Balance	Monthly Payment
Doctor	PAID OFF!	(Freed Up $200)
Credit Card 2	PAID OFF!	(Freed Up $100)
Credit Card 1	PAID OFF!	(Freed Up $150)
Car 2	PAID OFF!	(Freed Up $400)
Car 1	$2,700	$500
Student Loan	$11,250	$200
Total Debt	$13,950	$1,550

How exciting is this? You can see the light at the end of the tunnel! Now you only have two more debts left to pay-off. Since we just freed up $850, the other car payment will be gone in a blink of an eye. Here is what that will look like:

Debt Name	Balance	Monthly Payment
Doctor	PAID OFF!	(Freed Up $200)
Credit Card 2	PAID OFF!	(Freed Up $100)
Credit Card 1	PAID OFF!	(Freed Up $150)
Car 2	PAID OFF!	(Freed Up $400)
Car 1	$2,700	$1,350
Student Loan	$11,250	$200
Total Debt	$13,950	$1,550

DFD: 9 months

In two months, we won't have any car payments! Think how sweet it will feel to drive paid-in-full cars. Here is an updated look at our debt picture:

Debt Name	Balance	Monthly Payment
Doctor	PAID OFF!	(Freed Up $200)
Credit Card 2	PAID OFF!	(Freed Up $100)
Credit Card 1	PAID OFF!	(Freed Up $150)

Car 2	PAID OFF!	(Freed Up $400)
Car 1	PAID OFF!	(Freed Up $500)
Student Loan	$10,850	$1,550
Total Debt	$10,850	$1,550

At this point, your sole debt will be the student loan. You can apply $1,550 a month towards this. Talk about a big snowball! Doing this for another seven months will lead to DEBT FREE-DOM!

Let's take a minute to reflect. You started off with $52,700 in debt. Now, 34 months later, you are debt free! How amazing is that? What a great feeling this will be! No more late-night calls from collection agencies. You'll be able to peacefully shut your eyes at night. I told you that you can do this!

Unexpected Benefits Of Being Debt-Free

You can probably make a list of the great things that will happen when you no longer have any debt except the mortgage. There are also some other benefits of being debt-free you may not realize. Here are some of those:

A. You Will Sleep Better

I personally know some people who have a lot of debt. They do not sleep very well and wake up numerous times during the night. I am sure owing someone money contributes to their sleepless nights.

B. You Will Be Able To Give Money Away

It is great to be able to buy things and invest your money to have it grow, but being able to give money away might be the greatest reason to get out of debt. Imagine writing a $10,000 check to your church and it not bouncing! Think of one of the wealthiest people on Earth, Oprah Winfrey. She has made more money than you and I probably ever will. She can buy (and has probably bought) pretty much anything she wants. However, when she talks about what gives her great joy, it has nothing to do with anything she has bought for herself. One of Oprah's greatest joys is the school she started in South Africa. Material things come and go. Helping others can create a legacy that will last generations.

C. You Can Invest Like Never Before

When you are not paying someone else interest, you can use this money to earn interest for yourself by investing. This is known as compound interest. Compound interest can be thought of as earning interest on interest that has already been paid to you.

Here's an easy way to see the magic of compound interest. Let's say you invest $100 and this investment averages a 9% return a year. Because of compound interest, this money will double in eight years. The chart below shows you how this works.

Year	Money Earned from Interest	Total Amount of Money
0	$0.00	$100.00
1	$9.00 (9% of $100.00)	$109.00
2	$9.81 (9% of $109.00)	$118.81
3	$10.69 (9% of $118.81)	$129.50
4	$11.66 (9% of $129.50)	$141.16
5	$12.70 (9% of $141.16)	$153.86
6	$13.85 (9% of $153.86)	$167.71
7	$15.09 (9% of $167.71)	$182.80
8	$16.45 (9% of $182.80)	$199.26

Here is another neat way to see how compound interest works. If I asked which would you rather have: $1,000 right now or a penny that doubles in value every day for one month, which would you select? I am sure you probably see there is a catch to the question and will select the penny; to show you how right you are, this penny would be worth over $5 million after 30 days. Here's how:

Day	Amount
1	$0.01
2	$0.02
3	$0.04
4	$0.08
5	$0.16
6	$0.32
7	$0.64
8	$1.28
9	$2.56
10	$5.12
11	$10.24
12	$20.48
13	$40.96
14	$81.92
15	$163.84
16	$327.68
17	$655.36
18	$1,310.72
19	$2,621.44
20	$5,242.88
21	$10,485.76
22	$20,971.52
23	$41,943.04
24	$83,886.08
25	$167,772.16
26	$335,544.32
27	$671,088.64
28	$1,342,177.28
29	$2,684,354.56
30	$5,368,709.12

This is definitely an extreme example, but is meant to show you how fast something can compound. In addition to the quote

I shared earlier, Einstein had another opinion concerning compound interest. Rumor has it that he said the following, "Compound interest is the eighth wonder of the world. He who understands it, earns it ... he who doesn't ... pays it." It is pretty difficult to disagree with the man often referred to as the father of modern physics.

D. Your Spouse Will Be Happy

Tracy and I established our hopes and dreams—before we even got married. Because of this, we have always been on the same page when it comes to our finances. We have financial margin in place and this has strengthened our marriage in more ways than a savings account can show. With two daughters in various activities, our lives can be pretty hectic. Because our mortgage is our only debt, we never argue about money. This enables us to focus on other things which makes our bond that much stronger.

E. Paid-For-In Advance Vacations Are Amazing

Imagine having your summer vacation not follow you home in the form of credit card bills. I have paid for vacations using a credit card and for some upfront in cash. The ones I paid for with cash were much more relaxing and enjoyable than the ones I paid for using my credit card.

F. You Need To Earn Less To Maintain The Same Lifestyle

When you no longer are paying debt payments, you get to keep that money instead. Therefore, you do not need to make as much to maintain your current lifestyle. For instance, let's say you need $3,000 a month to live and cover your expenses. $500 of this is credit card debt payments. Once the debt is gone, you need only $2,500 to maintain the same lifestyle!

SCARY DEBT STATISTIC

The American Psychological Association conducts a yearly survey on stress in the United States. The 2014 survey, in which 54% of Americans said they had just enough or not enough money each month to meet their expenses, found money to be the country's No. 1 stressor. Seventy-two percent of adults reported feeling stressed about money at least some of the time, and nearly a quarter rated their stress as "extreme."

Wealthy Life Question

What is your DFD (Debt Freedom Date)? Write down your debts below and calculate your DFD.

Debt Name, Balance, Monthly Payment

Chapter 6

Financial Margin

Revenue is vanity ... Margin is sanity ... Cash is king
ANONYMOUS

The Climb Continues

Once you have passed Level 7 and eliminated all your debt except your mortgage, you move up to Level 8. Imagine how nice it is as you get closer to winning the game. You are going to find it a little easier from here on out because you are now going to increase your net worth with each level you pass.

In Level 8, you will increase your savings to cover at least three months of expenses. Once you pass this level, you will probably never repeat it. You will have enough financial margin to cover most of the everyday expenses and minor emergencies that life sometimes throws your way. In addition, after getting out of debt, you will never want to go back to owing someone else.

To show you why it will get a little easier, let's say you started The Game of Financial Freedom needing $3,000 a month to cover your living expenses. However, after paying off all of your non-house debt in Level 7, you only need $2,500 a month ($500 was going towards your debts). Way back in Level 5 you saved up one month of expenses so you already have $3,000 in your savings account. You now want to have enough savings to cover at least 3 months of expenses. This would be a grand total of

$7,500 (remember, because you paid off your debt, you only need $2,500 a month now). You need to add $4,500 to what you currently have saved. Because you are not paying $500 towards your debt anymore, you can pay yourself this amount every month. Do this for 9 months and you will have 3 months of expenses saved! This will cover unexpected emergencies and opportunities. While we are in Level 8, I want to go over why it is important to have savings.

The Importance of Saved Money

When we save money, we are sacrificing today so we will have money to spend in the future. It requires you to live differently than many people. Many have little or no money saved because putting money aside requires one to deny themselves something they really want right now, so that they have money available for later. To make it even more difficult, you often don't even know what that saved money will be used for. We live in a culture of "I see it, I want it, and I buy it" so it can be really difficult to put anything aside. Since this is the case, far too many spend their entire checks, and in some cases more than what they bring in. Here is some proof of that:

According to Bankrate's Financial Security Index poll:
- 23% of Americans have no emergency savings at all
- Another 22% said their emergency savings would not cover three months' worth of expenses
- Only 29% have six months' worth of expenses for use in an emergency, the minimum recommended by many financial planning experts (a)

So, according to this poll, a minority of Americans have an adequate amount of money saved to cover unexpected emergencies and/or opportunities. YIKES!

There are two basic ways you can save money: investing it in hopes that it will earn interest and grow (this is done in 6th, 9th and 11th levels in The Game of Financial Freedom) or placing it into a savings account that doesn't earn much interest but is there for protection, purchases, and opportunities. These are levels 5 and 8 in the Game of Financial Freedom. That is what we are going to focus on in this chapter.

Where Does It Go?

To begin, remember that we are not trying to earn a lot of interest on our emergency funds; funds for growth is the money you invest in 6th, 9th and 11th levels in The Game of Financial Freedom. An emergency fund should be in a place that is easily accessible, but not so easy that you will be tempted to spend it. You can simply use a money market savings account at your bank. Ally Bank and Capital One 360 also offer great savings accounts. This type of account allows you to write checks from it or transfer money online from it into your checking account with a few clicks.

How to Save

To be successful at saving money, consider employing a strategy known as "pay yourself first." You see, most of us pay ourselves last. We pay other people for all of our expenses and then have nothing left over for ourselves. Why do you think the government takes taxes out of our paychecks before we receive them? Could you imagine if they waited and asked us to pay them what we owe every April? As staggering as our national debt is, I am sure it would be much higher!

Establish an automatic transfer from your paycheck into your savings account. Pretend this money is not even there. Make it a habit to continuously save a set amount or percentage of your income and put this amount into a savings account every month; over time, you will have a huge umbrella to protect you during those rainy days!

Why Is It Important?

Saving is important for five main reasons. First, saving covers emergencies. It provides security for unexpected events like having a major repair or a sudden illness. This way you have money to draw from so that you can continue to advance through the Game of Financial Freedom. Second, when you continue to save, you should be able to buy a car, furniture, etc., without having to use credit and possibly pay interest on the purchase. Third, savings will enable you to pay for those known, upcoming non-monthly expenses. Fourth, savings can enable you to take advantage of opportunities that come your way and provide a pool of resources to make your hopes and dreams become a reality. Finally, savings provides protection in case you lose your job.

Five Ways a Savings Account Can Help You

1. Emergencies

No one expects something bad to happen but sometimes life throws us a curveball. I was reminded of this a few years ago. We were enjoying one of those picture-perfect fall family days. We decided to get some frozen yogurt. While we were enjoying our treats, our girls started doing gymnastics. Out of the blue, Ava slipped and broke her arm! We had to rush her to the local emergency room, and they had to put a cast on it. Even though we have good health insurance, we still had a co-pay of $150 for this ER visit. I definitely wasn't planning on this expense, but it was not a big deal because we had an emergency fund. It was such an emotional day (all parents know what I'm talking about when you can't make your baby feel better), and I am so glad we were able to solely focus on Ava and not stress about the bill.

2. Purchases

I know some people say they just have bad luck and something always seems to go wrong. The truth is, luck really has nothing to do with it. If you live in a house long enough, something will break. If you drive a car long enough, something will need to be repaired. If you have kids, they will break something: either an object or a body part. It is called life.

My family has experienced all of these firsthand. Our garage door suddenly stopped working. We had a repair company come out and we needed new springs and a few other things. The total came to a little over $900. Six months later, I needed repairs on my car that totaled $800. Three months after that, at the beginning of summer, our air conditioning unit went out and we had to purchase a new unit. That cost us $4,000. Then, one week later, Tracy's car needed repairs which totaled another $1,000! Because we had planned for such unexpected events and had ample savings, we were able to pay for these in cash and move on with our lives. There were no future credit card bills that would follow us for months; we simply wrote a check and were done with it.

I know many think that having payments is just a way of life. That does not have to be the case. If you build up your savings account, you can pay for most of your purchases outright and move on with your life.

3. Known Upcoming Non-Monthly Expenses (KUEs)

Saving money every month for your KUEs is something I learned from my friend Joe Sangl, President of I Was Broke. Now I'm Not. These can also be called budget-busters because that is exactly what they will do. These expenses seem to appear at the last minute and at the most inopportune times because we have not prepared for them even though we knew they were coming.

For instance, Christmas comes every December 25th without fail. However, many people fail to prepare for the expenses associated with this holiday and turn to debt to buy presents for their loved ones. This causes them to lose some, if not all, the progress they have made the previous eleven months of the year with their finances.

You can save for your KUEs by making them an "every paycheck" expense. The first step is to identify all of your upcoming non-monthly expenses. Here is a list of common KUEs:

- Real Estate Property Taxes
- Life Insurance Premiums
- Auto Insurance Premiums
- Car Repairs and Maintenance
- Home Repairs and Maintenance
- Health Club Fees
- Golf Club Fees
- Professional Organization Dues
- Vacations
- Income Taxes
- Weddings
- Christmas
- Birthdays
- Anniversaries
- Graduations
- College Expenses
- Car Replacement
- Furniture Replacement

This list could go and on. The most important thing to remember is these expenses are both KNOWN and UPCOMING. There should be no surprises. The great thing is that saving for these KUEs is not that difficult. You must have discipline to set aside money each paycheck but you will be so happy that you did.

For instance, let's say you plan to spend $1,200 on Christmas. If you save $100 a month starting in January, you will have $1,200 by December. Think about how nice it will be using CASH for Christmas! Because you saved for it in advance, this holiday won't follow you until the following June in the form of credit card bills!

Just like a mortgage company will put money for your property taxes and homeowner's insurance into an Escrow account, you can calculate the amount you need to save each paycheck for these expenses and create an Escrow account for them.

To show you an example, we are going to say you get paid once a month. You want to have the following amounts for your KUEs:

Christmas	$1,000
Vacation	$1,200
Property Taxes	$1,500
Health Insurance Deductible	$2,500
Car Repairs	$800

When we add these together, we get a grand total of $7,000. We take this $7,000 and divide it by 12, the number of paychecks you will receive in a year if you are paid monthly. This equals $583. Now we break this down into the KUE sub-categories we have listed. So every month we put $83 into our Christmas Fund, $100 into our Vacation Fund, $125 into our Property Taxes Fund, $208 into our Health Insurance Deductible Fund and $66 into our Car Repairs Fund.

See how this can help you? By turning these non-monthly expenses into monthly ones, you have dramatically lessened the impact they will have on your budget. For instance, when it is time for vacation, you will already have $1,200 saved for it!

Here are some tips when calculating your KUEs:
- Recalculate these at least once per year
- Don't forget to add long-term expenses such as weddings and vehicle replacement
- Make your savings for these automatic

4. Funding Hopes and Dreams/Taking Advantage of Opportunities

I do feel people are correct when they say that the rich get richer and the poor get poorer. First, rich people continue to do the same actions that helped them accumulate money in the first place and poor people continue to do the same things that made them broke.

Another reason this occurs is that rich people have money set aside to take advantage of opportunities that arise. I was reminded of this when I decided to publish my first book, *How to Survive (and Perhaps Thrive) on a Teacher's Salary*. At that point in my life, I was a school teacher and that was it. I was not a writer in any way, shape, or form. As I mentioned before, I had to pay almost $4,000 to have my first book published; but it was well worth the cost.

My books have given me many opportunities. There are also other doors out there that I have no clue exist yet, but will possibly open for me because of what I have been able to accomplish. However, none of this would have ever happened if I had not had any money to invest in myself. I have heard luck defined as when opportunity meets preparation. Please start preparing your savings account so that you, too, can take advantage of the opportunities that will come your way.

5. Changing Jobs/Job Loss

I felt a calling to help others manage their money better. A couple of years ago I was offered the chance to do this. I actually took a slight cut in pay from what I was making teaching, but was so glad that I was able to take advantage of this opportunity. I had some positive results and was rewarded with a greater than 40 percent raise before a year ended. However, we never got used to living up to this salary.

The following year I was offered the chance to help others manage money in churches throughout the country but this job had one catch: I had to take greater than a 25 percent pay cut! Because Tracy and I had never gotten used to living up to my higher salary, I was able to take this job that I felt He was calling me to do.

After having this job for seven months, I was laid off. The company did not grow as expected and I was no longer needed. This is where our savings helped us so much. I cannot begin to explain how difficult this was to my psyche. As a man, I feel like I need to be the provider for my family. Because this is the case, I was ready to take the first opportunity presented to me. Two days after being let go, I had a job offer to teach at a school that was over an hour from home. I was strongly considering it, but Tracy reminded me that we had savings in place and I could take a little longer to make a decision. She knew driving this far every day would not be a good fit for our family. Having savings in place enabled me to wait for a job that I was better suited for.

A Final Thought on Saving

For an even greater incentive to save, compare the results of spending $100 more than you earn each month for ten years with spending $100 less than you earn each month for ten years. By spending $100 more each month, you will be in the hole $12,000 before interest is even calculated; spend $100 less and you will possess $12,000 before you total the interest earned: a staggering difference of $24,000 at the end of ten years! The difference between sinking into debt and walking on the firm ground of savings is a matter of a few dollars a day.

Wealthy Life Questions

1. How much money do you need in savings to cover three months of living expenses to help you avoid future debt?

$____ X 3 months = $_____

2. How much should you save from each paycheck in order to fund your KUEs?

Chapter 7

Lose the Mortgage, Too

"Bad debt is debt that makes you poorer. I count the mortgage on my home as bad debt, because I'm the one paying on it."

ROBERT KIYOSAKI

Before you continue your Debt Freedom March, let's take a minute to revisit The Game of Financial Freedom. Here are the levels:

Power-up	Know Your Why/Set Goals
Level 1	Get Health, Auto, and Homeowner's Insurance
Level 2	Get Disability Insurance
Level 3	Get Life Insurance
Level 4	Get a Will
Level 5	Save One Month of Expenses
Level 6	Invest $100/Month for Retirement
Level 7	Eliminate All Debt Except the Mortgage
Level 8	Save at Least Three Months of Expenses
Level 9	Invest 15 percent of Your Salary
Level 10	Pay off Your Mortgage
Level 12	Invest 30 percent of Your Salary
Level 12	Do Whatever You Want/Live a Prosperous Life

We start focusing on paying off the mortgage in 10th level. If you are in this level, you have at least three months of expenses saved, are investing 15 percent of your salary for retirement, and have no debt except your mortgage. Now we can start attacking that last debt: your mortgage! In fact, this might not take as long as you think.

Let's use the numbers from Chapter 5. You started off with $52,700 in total debt and were paying $1,550/month towards this debt. Once that debt was eliminated, you used this $1,550 to build your savings to cover at least three months of expenses (Level 8 in The Game of Financial Freedom). After this is done, you can use a portion of the $1,550 to invest 15 percent of your salary and use the remaining to pay off your mortgage. This can happen sooner than you ever imagined.

Buying A House – The Mortgage

For most of us, a mortgage will be the largest debt we carry in our lives. Purchasing a house makes financial sense for a number of reasons. Over a good period of time, real estate and home values normally appreciate. However, like investing in the stock market, this increase is not a given every year.

If you plan on living somewhere for a short period of time (less than five years), it might make more sense to rent so you will not have to worry about selling your house when it is time to move. A second advantage of owning a home is, once you pay it off, you will have a place to live rent-free for the remainder of your time in that house. In addition, if you do decide to sell and move somewhere else, you will have equity in this house and, generally speaking, make tax-free money from this sale.

To briefly illustrate this, suppose a person decides to rent rather than purchase a home. His rent is $750/month. This adds up to a total of $9,000 a year spent on housing. The person lives there for ten years and then decides to move. He will have paid $90,000 in rent with nothing to show for it. Suppose this same person purchased the house instead for $125,000, put 20% down and took out a 15-year loan with a 4% interest rate. Using these terms, his mortgage would be $100,000. This would leave him with the same monthly payment – about $750 (not including taxes and insurance) – as the rent. After ten years he decides to move. If the house had increased in value by 1% each year, it would be valued at $138,077 after ten years. Because he had been making monthly payments on this debt, he now owes only $40,164 on this loan. Even with a real estate selling charge of 6%, he would walk away with $90,000!

An argument I have heard against owning a home is that it would be wiser to rent an inexpensive house and save the money that you would have spent on an expensive mortgage payment. It is hard to argue with the math. If one could rent a home for $500 a month instead of paying a mortgage payment of $1,000, it would free up $500 a month. This money could be used to build up the emergency fund or invest. While the math is clear, do you know many people who would actually save or invest ALL of this extra money? Even with the best intentions, something always seems to come up, and we find ways to spend this "extra" money. In the long run, most people would spend this money on something that would be long gone after a few months.

According to the Bureau of Labor Statistics' Consumer Expenditure Survey, housing accounted for roughly one-third of American households' spending in 2018. (a) Many Realtors suggest that one can spend one-third of his/her gross pay on housing. That does hold true for many that are in the low-moderate income bracket. There are many that gross around $50,000 a year and search for homes in the $150,000 range. However, this logic seems to break down as we make more money. There are some who make $100,000 a year yet search for $400,000 homes. It seems as we make more, we spend a greater percentage of our income on our home. This limits one's options in life. Some choose to live so large that they have no money left over to take vacations, go out to eat, or even furnish their home. I point this out in case you fall into that category. If so, downsizing can be a great way to boost your financial situation.

Lose the Mortgage

Now that we have discussed the reasons people have mortgages, we are going to look at ways to get rid of this large debt. This is where the fun really begins! Look around your home, in your garage, and out your backdoor. Imagine the feeling of owning it all, free and clear. How would you feel?

Many people assume they will always have a house payment and don't realize how much interest they are paying on their loans. Let's say you buy a house for $150,000. You make a down payment of $30,000 and take out a 30-year mortgage for $120,000 with a 5% interest rate. If you made the regular monthly payment, your $150,000 house will have cost you $261,840 when all is said and done!

Here are a few ways you can pay off your mortgage faster:

1. Pay Extra

You can sign up for a 30-year loan and promise yourself that you will pay extra each month towards this loan. If you are serious about paying your home off early, this is probably not the best option. Most of us make promises we cannot keep. We might have the best intentions to pay extra each month but then something comes up—Valentine's Day in February, summer vacation in July, Christmas in December—and we find we need this "extra" money for something other than the house.

2. Make Biweekly Payments

If you do have a 30-year loan, you could sign up to make biweekly payments instead of a monthly payment. These biweekly payments will be half of your monthly payment but you will actually make an extra payment each year. Here is how this works. Let's say your monthly payment is $1,000. You would pay $12,000 each year towards your mortgage: 12 (months in a year) times $1,000 (monthly payment) = $12,000. If you used the biweekly approach, you'll pay $500 (half of the monthly $1,000 payment) every two weeks. There are 52 weeks in a year so you'll make 26 half payments. $500 times 26 equals $13,000; thus, you will make one extra $1,000 payment each year. This can trim anywhere from five to seven years off your 30-year loan depending on your interest rate. One warning about this approach; be careful your mortgage company doesn't charge a fee for this. Some of them try to slip this in so just make sure yours does not.

3. Refinance

Perhaps the easiest way to pay off your loan is to refinance. As I write, interest rates are still historically low. My family moved from Florida to Georgia in the summer of 2006. We selected a 30-year loan. When interest rates dropped to record lows in 2013, we refinanced. We were able to lower our rate by three full points and reduced our term to ten years. We paid around $275 more each month compared to our original loan but built up more equity and were on track to pay it off a lot sooner and save almost $75,000 in interest!

In fact, if all you did was simply lower your interest rate by 1% on a 30-year, $100,000 mortgage, you would save over $600 per year! You could apply this savings to your principal and pay off your mortgage a lot sooner.

Arguments Against Paying Off Your Mortgage

There are some who argue against paying off the mortgage. Here are a few common arguments:

1. You Will Lose The Deduction On Your Taxes

One argument I have heard against paying off your mortgage early is that you won't be able to take the home mortgage interest deduction and reduce your taxable income. First, in order to claim this credit, you must itemize your deductions. Most Americans take the standard deduction so this wouldn't even matter to them. (b)

Let's pretend you are not in the majority and itemize your deductions. You are married and, between you and your spouse, earn between $77,401 to $165,000 a year. This would put you in the 22% income tax bracket. Suppose you have a 30-year, $200,000 mortgage with a 5% interest rate. In the first year, you would pay approximately $10,000 in interest (5% of $200,000 is $10,000). Now for your big tax write-off. Your taxable income will lower by $10,000. Since you're in the 22% tax bracket, this deduction will lower the amount you owe in taxes by $2,200 (22% of $10,000 equals $2,200). So, if you think you should keep your mortgage because of this deduction, you are basically saying you should pay $10,000 a year in interest to your mortgage company so that you can reduce the amount you owe Uncle Sam by $2,200. Now I am not a mathematical genius but paying $10,000 to save $2,200 doesn't make much sense to me. If this sounds good to you, please send me your contact information, and I will gladly write you a check for $2,200 in exchange for $10,000!

2. You Should Invest The Extra Money Instead Of Paying It Towards The Mortgage

Another argument I have heard against paying off a mortgage early is that one could invest this money and earn more in the stock market. That is hard to argue against because, historically speaking, it is accurate. If your mortgage rate is 5% and you pay it off early you will, in essence, be earning 5% a year, as you will no longer be paying a lender 5%; this money will remain in your bank account. The stock market has historically averaged more than 5% annual growth so, mathematically, paying extra towards your mortgage instead of investing this amount seems unwise. Here is where we have to look at the bigger picture.

If this is the case, why don't more people take out a home equity loan and invest it in the stock market? One could borrow money at a 5% set interest rate and earn more on this same money by investing it—sounds like a no-brainer to me. However, most people will not do this because they don't view their house as just an investment—it is a huge part of who they are.

While you could invest this money, imagine the feeling of owning all of your possessions! The grass in your backyard feels a lot different when you own it.

Let's Do The Math

To show you how this looks with real numbers, let's use the before-mentioned numbers using two different terms: a 30-year and a 15-year mortgage.

30-Year Mortgage

You recently purchased a $150,000 house and put 20% ($30,000) down on it. You then took out a 30-year, 5% interest rate loan for $120,000. Your monthly payment (excluding taxes and insurance) would be $644.19. This would total $7,730.28 a year. Multiply this by 30 years and you would get a grand total of $231,908.40. Add the $30,000 you used as your down payment and the total amount you will have paid on that $150,000 house will be $261,908.40. I bet you didn't hear that from the mortgage company! Let's see how we can pay the house off a lot faster.

Once again, we will use the numbers from Chapter 5. After eliminating your debt, you had $1,550 freed up. You then used this money to build up your savings and then moved to level 9 in The Game of Financial Freedom: invest 15 percent of your salary for long-term dreams. We will say the amount invested was $625. That leaves $925 per month remaining. Let's apply this to the mortgage.

By adding $925 to your monthly mortgage payment of $644.19 and applying it to the principal, you will pay off your mortgage in 7 years, 7 months and save over $87,000 in interest! Now let's try this approach with a shorter-term mortgage.

15-Year Mortgage

When it comes to purchasing a house, I strongly encourage you to consider a 15-year loan. The monthly payments will be higher, but you will own your home outright in half the time compared to a 30-year loan. This frees up 30 percent of your income to invest and do whatever you want.

Let's use the same numbers. Instead of a 30-year loan, you took out a 15-year, 4.5% interest rate loan for $120,000. Notice, the interest rate is lower than the one with the 30-year loan because, by taking on a shorter term loan, you are usually able to get a better rate.

Your monthly payment (excluding taxes and insurance) would be $917.99. This would total $11,015.88 a year. Multiply this by 15 years and, it equals $165,238.20. Add the $30,000 you used as your down payment and the total amount you will have paid on the $150,000 house will be $195,238.20! So let's pause a minute and think about this. Obtaining a 15-year mortgage instead of a 30-year, will save you over $66,000 in interest when all is said and done. Yes, you will be paying a little over $273 more each month, but you will own the house free and clear 15 years sooner and save a lot of money.

It gets even better. Add the same $925 freed up from debt to your monthly payment. This makes your monthly payment $1,842.99/month. Doing this will enable you to pay off your mortgage in just 6 years, 9 months! In addition, the total amount you will have paid on that $150,000 house would only be $179,282. Can you imagine? In less than seven years, you will own your house outright!

Almost Sounds Too Good To Be True

Let's take a look to see how you have changed your life. You entered The Game of Financial Freedom a little over 9 years ago. You had no goals, did not have disability or life insurance, had nothing in savings, were not saving anything for retirement, had $52,700 in debt and owed $120,000 on your mortgage.

You now have no debt; you are investing 15 percent of your salary; you have at least three months of expenses in your savings account; and you have a paid-off mortgage. Wow! Think about your future now. How bright will it be?

You will now be on Level 11 in The Game of Financial Freedom: Invest 30 percent of Your Salary for Long-Term Dreams. I bet if someone had told you a few years ago that you would be in the position to invest 30 percent of your salary, you would have thought they were talking about someone else. But here you are. In fact, you could easily invest more than 30 percent and not even really feel it!

Using the aforementioned numbers, we are assuming you make $50,000 a year. You started investing 15 percent of your income in Level 9, so we need to invest another 15 percent of your salary to get to 30 percent. To do this, we would need to invest an additional $625 a month.

We will say you had the 15-year mortgage just discussed. After paying off your debt and building your savings, you were paying $1,842.99 on your mortgage every month. After the mortgage is gone, you could invest an additional $625 every month and still have $1,200 left over! I know we are focused on getting rid of debt, but let's take a look at what investing this amount could accomplish. If you were investing 30 percent of a $50,000 annual salary, that would equate to $1,250 every month. To put an age on it, let's say you started doing this amount at age 40. Remember, you have already been investing 15 percent of your salary for a few years and your retirement account is worth

$40,000 when you start investing $1,250 each month.

If you had $40,000 in your retirement account, invested $1,250 every month starting at age 40, averaged 8 percent growth per year on this and did this for 25 years, how much do you think you would have? If you guessed over $1.4 million, you are the winner! Talk about being able to do pretty much do whatever you want. See, you can do this!

Wealthy Life Questions

What is the interest rate you are currently paying on your mortgage? How much total do you owe on it? How many years do you have left?

If you applied the money from your Level 7 debt payments to your mortgage, how soon would you pay it off?

Chapter 8

Speed Up Your Debt Freedom March

"In skating over thin ice our safety is in our speed."

RALPH WALDO EMERSON

Now that you know exactly what to do to get rid of all of your debt, I'm sure you are excited to get started. In fact, imagining what it will be like to live a wealthy life probably has you wishing there was a way you could speed up the amount of time it will take to get there. Well, have I got some GREAT news for you! Here are some ways to do so.

8 Ways to Speed Up Your Debt Freedom March

1. Reduce Interest Rates On Debt

Unfortunately, once you get into debt, it can be really difficult to get out. This is because some of your payment is not touching the principal at all; it is only going towards interest. If you have a credit card with a high interest rate, look into transferring it to a 0% interest one. This is called a 0% balance transfer card. Is your mortgage rate too high? Visit www.bankrate.com to see a list of 0 percent APR credit cards along with current mortgage rates. Spending a few hours lowering the amount you are paying in interest can greatly accelerate your Debt Freedom March!

2. Get A Raise

Are you being paid what you are worth? I know most of us feel we deserve more but go to www.payscale.com or www.salary.com to compare your pay to others in your field. Then, ask your boss for a meeting and ask what he/she considers outstanding performance for someone in your position and how you can earn the maximum pay. Finally, show how you have added value to your company and continue to keep track of this—the more specific, the better. Obtaining a raise and adding this income to your Debt Freedom March can greatly decrease the amount of time you will need to complete it.

3. Tax Refund

I know there are some who think it is a bad idea to get a tax refund because you are basically loaning money to the government interest-free. While there is some truth to this, I would much rather get a refund than owe the government more; I have been in both of these situations. You can even view your tax refund as a form of disciplined savings. In addition, if you use your refund to pay off debt, the interest you "earn" by eliminating this debt will far outpace any interest this money would have earned in a bank account.

4. Performance Bonus

An unexpected (or expected) bonus at work can be applied to your debt to speed up your Debt Freedom March. Once you eliminate this debt, any future bonuses can be used for fun stuff: those dreams and goals you listed in the beginning of The Game of Financial Freedom.

5. Found Money From Better Budgeting

In a bit, we are going to go over some specific ways you can save money. As you plan your spending each month, you will identify expenses that can be reduced or eliminated. You can use this money to pay off your debt faster.

6. Sell Some Stuff

Many of us fill all of our available space with stuff. Tracy and I started our married lives in a two-bedroom apartment. After two years, it was full. We then moved to a two-bedroom house that was more than double the size of that apartment. In a couple of years, it was full. We now live in a larger house, and you guessed it, it is full! We have a house for our cars (a garage) that we can't park in sometimes because we have stuff in it. I know some people who have so much stuff they need a storage unit in addition to a house! You might be experiencing the same thing. If you feel you just have too much stuff, have a garage sale or sell it on Ebay and use the proceeds to pay off your debt.

7. Work Overtime

I am not saying to do this forever, but acquiring more income can help you get to your Debt Freedom Date much sooner. As a teacher, I worked summer school and in the after school program to earn a little more. While there were some days I was extremely tired, this extra income really helped us. As an added bonus, you are not spending when you are working!

8. Work an Extra Job

I know some may not have the opportunity to work overtime at their current place of employment. If this is the case, you might want to consider working a second job. If you are passionate about a specific product or hobby, you may even consider starting a side business. You never know where this passion could lead you. For example, I had a passion for personal finance and wrote books to help others with this. I don't make a lot from these books but every little bit helps.

Apply these tips to your situation to speed up your Debt Freedom March.

SCARY DEBT STATISTIC

In a 2014 Pew survey, 55% of Americans spend
as much as they make each month or more.

Ways To Save Money (so you can eliminate debt faster)

There are two basic ways to make more money: either
increase your income or eliminate some of your expenses. I
listed some ways to increase your income above. Here are some
specific ways to save money.

1. Stop Paying Credit Card Interest

The only thing worse than buying something you can't
afford is buying something you don't have the money for and
then end up paying interest for it. Let's say you decide to upgrade
your living room and buy a new television set, couch, and
recliner. The total cost is $5,000 and you purchase these items
on a credit card with an 18.9 percent interest rate. The minimum
payment is 2 percent of the balance, which would start at
$100/month. If you continued to just make this minimum
monthly payment, it would take you over 30 years to pay off,
and you would have spent over $19,000 doing so. This is almost
four times the purchase price!

2. Switch Cell Phone Plans

Tracy and I both went a long time without smartphones.
When we finally upgraded into the 21st Century, we decided to
be as smart about this as possible. Instead of locking into a
two-year plan, we both bought used iPhones and signed up for
WalMart's Straight Talk plan. We paid a total of $90 a month for
our phones combined and had the same service that friends of
ours had. Yet some of them paid in excess of $200.

One of my employers paid for my cell phone. After leaving the company, I took over the payment. I stayed with the same carrier to make the transition easier, but for pretty much the same plan I had had with Straight Talk, I was paying over $100 a month! This was more than double what I had been paying before so I quickly switched back to Straight Talk; but, to add a little more insult to injury, I had to pay a $175 cancellation fee. Lesson learned!

Ten years ago many of us did not even have cell phones and got along just fine. Now some pay over $200 a month for their phone plans. If you are looking to cut costs, this may be an area where that you can save some serious cash.

3. Stop Paying Full Price at the Grocery Store

Tracy really got serious about using coupons in 2010 and the results have been great; since then we have saved over $8,000 by using coupons and shopping for deals. She does not go overboard, and we will never have our own reality show about couponing, but it just shows that shopping smart can help stretch your paycheck. Here are some tips to help you save at the grocery store:

Leave The Spender At Home
In most relationships, there is a spender and saver. The spender seems to be able to spend money on items the saver has never even thought about. You can send the spender to the grocery store with a specific list and they still come home with much more. Don't set yourself up for failure: let the spender stay home.

Shop With A List
It's called impulse buying for a reason. We have a tough time resisting the temptation to purchase extras when shop-

ping. Without a list you will buy items that you simply do not need. Grocery stores are masterful at placing tempting items at the ends of aisles to get your attention. Even worse is when you forget to purchase the actual item you went to the store for in the first place. If you are cooking at home, pre-plan a rough menu and make a list before going grocery shopping. Getting all the food you need in one trip can help you avoid another unnecessary trip and the temptations that go along with that.

Shop The Sales
In addition to using coupons, you can also shop sales. Most grocery stores have sales cycles in which certain items go on sale every few weeks. Take some time to note this and plan your spending in advance. Do this and you will never pay full price again!

Don't Shop Hungry
Going to the store after a long day of work is self-sabotage. When you are tired and hungry you will be tempted to buy the first thing that smells good. Tracy usually goes shopping on a non-workday morning after eating breakfast. As an added bonus, the store is less crowded!

Leave The Kids At Home
If you have children, this tip is pretty obvious. When Tracy brings Ava or Ella with her, she **always** spends more. Let the kids stay home with the spender and it will be much easier to stick with the list.

4. When Eating Out, Stop Splurging On Appetizers and Drinks
The portions at restaurants seem to increase as fast as our country's average waist size. If you are like me, you usually need

a to-go box because you cannot eat your entire meal. Why pay more money for an appetizer when all it does is take up space in your belly before your meal is even brought out? In addition, soft drinks and sweet tea can now cost over $2. If you have a family of four, that is over $8 for drinks alone. Order water instead, and you can save lots of money. I have a friend who used to pay his children a dollar if they ordered water instead of a soda. He taught them a lesson and saved money at the same time.

5. Stop Paying Overdraft Fees

There is truly no excuse for this. If you balance your checkbook and spend less than you earn, you will never have to spend any of your hard-earned money on these expensive fees.

6. Stop Signing Up For Quick Delivery

In the instant gratification days we live in, many people order things online and have these items shipped by priority mail. If you cannot wait the standard shipping time frame (usually between 5-10 days) for something to arrive, you may want to consider doing without that item completely.

7. Don't Buy Designer Kids' and Baby Clothes

Until your child stops growing inches every year, there is no need to buy the newest fashion clothes for him/her. Why waste $25 on a shirt he will wear two or three times? This is especially true when it comes to dressing our babies. Why spend a lot of money on something that only gets spit up on?

8. Re-Think Your Gym Membership

I am all for exercising (and go to the gym myself) but many people have gym memberships and the last time they went to the gym was six months ago. It is very easy to buy into the hype and set a New Year's resolution to lose weight and join a gym.

Unfortunately, after enthusiasm wanes around Valentine's Day, the monthly dues do not stop coming out of your bank account. If you want to get in shape, you can do many healthy things for little cost. Before joining a gym, I ran nine half-marathons and the only thing it cost me was the price of good running shoes.

9. Ditch Your Satellite Television and Premium Cable Packages

Don't get me wrong, I enjoy watching television, especially sports. I even order the NFL package so that I can watch my beloved Miami Dolphins every fall Sunday. However, some of us have over 200 channels and only watch a few of them. If you are looking for ways to save some serious money, this might be a good place to start. Sure, you may not be able to keep up with those "real" housewives but, now that a few of them have filed for bankruptcy, who would want to anyway?

10. Stop Having Car Payments

According to Experian Automotive, the average monthly payment on a new vehicle in the third quarter of 2018 was $530. The average used-car payment was $381. (a)

As you can easily see, driving a used car can save you some serious money. Even better, drive a car as long as possible. I drove a car for over 16 years but finally had to get a different one recently because it died (yes, had to have it towed to the car dealership to trade it in!) one morning on my way to work. However, I did not have a car payment for over 14 years.

11. Quit Buying Name-Brand Paper Products

Think about it: you use paper towels, napkins, and plates only once (even I don't re-use these!). Spending more for the name-brand version of these products is a big waste. Buy the generic brand instead and save.

12. Start Using K-Cups Instead of Regular Coffee

I know many people now use Keurigs or a similar type of machine to brew coffee. For convenience, many use k-cups. Instead, purchase the filters for these machines and buy regular coffee. Yes, you have to clean these out, but the time is definitely worth the cost. I priced the cost of k-cups compared to ground coffee and was very surprised at how much more you will pay when buying individual pods. This was the same exact brand and style of coffee. You would pay $2.02 per ounce for the k-cups compared with $0.07 an ounce for the ground coffee. That is a savings of $1.95 per ounce!

13. Brown Bag Your Lunch

I know it can be a challenge to plan ahead and pack your lunch, but it can save you a lot of money. Let's say you eat lunch out every day during the work week. We will keep it cheap and say you eat fast food and spend only $5 per meal. Most of us won't miss that $5 or even think twice about spending it. Well, $5 per day Monday to Friday equals $25 a week, $100 a month and $1,300 a year. That's a lot of money!

14. Avoid The Box Office

I realize going out to the movies can be a fun way to spend an evening, but it is definitely costly. If you are going to the movie theater twice each month, you are spending a lot of money in exchange for a few hours of entertainment. We are not even including the snacks because who can go to the movies and resist the $8 bucket of popcorn and $5 soda? Wait a few months until the movie comes out at Redbox and pop your own popcorn at home. You get to watch the same film and eat the same food at a greatly reduced price.

15. Get New Home and Auto Insurance Quotes

This is often an overlooked expense that can result in huge

savings! I know from firsthand experience how much this can save you. I recently got new quotes on my insurance. I had not even thought about this since we moved to Georgia years ago. I met with a local insurance agent for one hour and saved over $1,200/year on my homeowner's insurance and almost $300/year on my car insurance! Get new quotes on these every two years.

16. Iron Your Own Clothes

This may not work for everyone, but ironing your own clothes instead of using a dry cleaner can save you some money. I can honestly say I have never had anything dry cleaned. It does take me some time to iron my shirts but I usually just let them pile. When there is a game on that I want to watch, I iron while I watch.

17. Save On Sporting Events

Sporting events can be an expensive venture. I do not go to live games often but every year for Mother's Day, I brave (pun intended) the Atlanta traffic and take my mom to watch the Dodgers play the Braves (she is a huge L.A. Dodger fan). I use the website www.scorebig.com and save on the price of our tickets. They offer up to 60% savings on certain tickets. This helps lessen the blow of spending $6 on a hot dog.

18. Don't Buy Expensive Razors

Another convenient way to save is to purchase razors from www.dollarshaveclub.com. I signed up for their Humble Twin Razor and receive 5 cartridges every month for just $3. The cartridges I used before cost me $2.25 each. If you do not shave much, you can even adjust how often you receive refills and have them delivered every other month.

19. Kids Eat Free

You can save serious money by choosing to eat at home but sometimes we choose to give ourselves (or, in my case, my wife) a break from cooking. If you have children and are planning to eat out, check out www.outtoeatwithkids.com. This site lists restaurants near you where kids eat free or at a reduced cost.

20. Dollar Store Shopping

Many have great intentions when shopping at these types of stores but end up walking out with a bunch of junk we really should not have bought. Despite that, you can really save when purchasing certain items from these types of stores. These include cleaning supplies, birthday cards, coloring books, wrapping paper, and party supplies. Just remember to stick with your list and don't let those shiny objects jump into your cart.

21. Drink Tap Water

A final way to save is to drink tap water. According to a Washington Post report, Americans drink an average of 270 bottles of water each year. (b)

If the price of a bottle of water was $1.00, a family of four would spend over $1,000 a year—on water!

For more tips on saving money, please visit my website www.wealthyteacher.weebly.com and fill out the contact form. I will then send you my free ebook *Save Over $30,000 This Year – 145 Tips To Help You Save Money Starting Today*. Now, you probably will not be able to use every tip but I can almost guarantee you will be able to find enough to offset the cost of this book!

I know, all work and no play makes Jack a dull boy. I completely get it and am not saying you have to utilize every cost-cutting item. But applying some of them can lead to some serious savings which can be redirected to paying off your debt much quicker so that you can experience a wealthy life.

Most of us can't have it all. If you don't want to cancel your satellite or cable package, that is fine. However, cut back in another area. Every financial action has a financial consequence. The lack of thinking about the consequences is what gets so many into financial trouble. If I make $50,000 a year, there is no way I can truly afford a $300,000 house. I don't care how much I qualify for—I cannot afford it!

I will never forget explaining this concept to Ava. Before attending elementary school, Ava mostly stayed home and Tracy watched her. She did go to a friend's house occasionally, but Tracy and I were friends with these children's parents and most of them lived like we did and did not buy a lot of toys for their children, as the budget didn't allow it. Elementary school opened Ava's eyes to how others lived. One day after entering kinder-garten, she came home with a great question. We were in her room and she asked, "Dad, can we move to a bigger house? Most of the kids in my class talk about how big their houses are and some even have extra rooms to put all their toys in." What a great teaching moment! I told her we could absolutely move but a few things would change. First, Ava liked having Tracy waiting at home for her every day after school. Well, that would have to change because Tracy would have to get a job so we could afford a bigger house. Ava also loved having her daddy teach at the same school she attended (I did, too!). If we moved to a bigger house, that would change, too, because I would have to get a higher paying job and leave teaching. Finally, even though she would have a bigger house and possibly more toys to play with, Ava would not be home as much because Tracy and I would have to work longer. She would be placed into the after-school program, and we would pick her up after 5:00 most days. After explaining these consequences to her, Ava replied, "Dad, I think we have it pretty good."

Sure, there are times I wish I had nicer stuff. Like most people, if I see someone pull up next to me in a shiny new BMW, of course I want it! I can have it, but something would have to change because of that decision. Since the day I married Tracy, I have not seen one object that made me want to change the way we are living. This all comes back to the beginning, Powering-up, in The Game of Financial Freedom. We have goals in place we are working towards. Accomplishing these goals means much more than any shiny piece of metal ever will.

Wealthy Life Question

What is one action you can take right now to save money and speed up your Debt Freedom March?

Conclusion

"Take the first step in faith. You don't have to see the
whole staircase, just take the first step."
MARTIN LUTHER KING, JR.

A Wealthy Life

Earlier in this book, I described a wealthy life as being able to do what you have been called to do no matter the cost or how much you can make by doing it. This definition recently became a reality for me in a way I never could have imagined.

Pop

In August, 2017, I had just started a new teaching position. After the fourth day of school I was driving home and got a horrible call on my phone: my dad, who we called Pop, had had a stroke that morning. When my mom got home from work that afternoon, she found him sitting in his chair, unable to move.

Just three weeks before this we were on a family vacation and he rode a bike six miles. He was only 60 years old! In a blink of an eye he went from being like you and me to being confined to a wheelchair, wearing briefs, and eating via a feeding tube. He needed assistance with anything he did.

Pop spent two months in rehabilitation and then came home. My mom needed assistance with his care so my entire family moved in with them. Luckily they had an upstairs suite so we all just lived there and helped care for him. We all continued to work and balanced our schedules so either Tracy, my mom, or I was at home to care for him.

This got to be really difficult so I approached my principal about working part-time. She agreed (she is an awesome person) and, right before Christmas break, I started working 7:00-11:00. I would then come home and take Pop to his therapies and work on the exercises they told us to do.

Tracy and I had planned on moving back to our house after Christmas but my mom still needed assistance with him so we made the decision to sell our house and move in with them. Around this time, I also asked Him for some direction. I planned on returning to teaching full-time the following year so my mom would have to hire a full-time caretaker for my dad (she was only 60 years old and needed to continue working for insurance and her retirement). I decided to resign from teaching to stay home full-time and take care of Pop.

Towards the beginning of summer, Pop was complaining of shortness of breath. We took him to the doctor and his lungs were filling with fluid; he was silently aspirating. There was nothing that could be done to reverse this. We did all we could with therapy. We all decided to have him come home with Hospice care.

A few weeks later, Pop passed away. It was the worst day of my life but, at the same time, kind of magical. When he passed, he was surrounded with nothing but love. His five grandchildren, two daughters-in-law, two sons, and wife were all with him. When I visited him in the hospital, I walked by numerous rooms that contained very sick patients. Many of these patients never had any visitors. How sad is that? Some could have been millionaires, yet in the end, what did this money do for them? My dad didn't have a million dollars but he was much wealthier than any of these people.

In addition, I realized how lucky I was to be able to take care of him. It was like the circle of life. I remember sitting by his bed on my last Father's Day with him. I knew at that point in time that the end was getting close and I just thanked God for giving me this opportunity.

None of this would have happened if Tracy and I had not managed our money well. If we were living paycheck-to-paycheck and had a lot of debt, there is no way we could have done what we did. Taking care of Pop added nothing to my net worth but it gave me more wealth than anything else in my life!

The Professor

I know it can be really discouraging to try and get our finances on track. We have jobs to pay the bills, meals to cook, and events to attend. When it seems like you just don't have enough time in the day to accomplish all that needs to be done, here is a story that shows us what is really important:

A professor stood before his philosophy class and had some items in front of him. When the class began, he wordlessly picked up a very large and empty mayonnaise jar and proceeded to fill it with golf balls. He then asked the students if the jar was full. They agreed that it was. The professor then picked up a box of pebbles and poured them into the jar. He shook the jar lightly. The pebbles rolled into the open areas between the golf balls. He then asked the students again if the jar was full. They agreed it was.

The professor next picked up a box of sand and poured it into the jar. Of course, the sand filled up everything else. He asked once more if the jar was full. The students responded with a unanimous "yes."

The professor then produced two cups of coffee from under the table and poured the entire contents into the jar, effectively filling the empty space between the sand. The students laughed.

"Now," said the professor as the laughter subsided, "I want you to recognize that this jar represents your life. The golf balls are the important things—your family, your children, your health, your friends, and your favorite passions—and if everything else was lost and only they remained, your life would still be full. The pebbles are the other things that matter like your job, your house, and your car. The sand is everything else: the small stuff. "If you put the sand into the jar first," he continued, "there is no room for the pebbles or the golf balls. The same goes for life. If you spend all your time and energy on the small stuff you will never have room for the things that are important to you. "Pay attention to the things that are critical to your happiness. Play with your children. Take time to get medical checkups. Take your spouse out to dinner. Play another 18. There will always be time to clean the house and fix the disposal. Take care of the golf balls first: the things that really matter. Set your priorities. The rest is just sand."

One of the students raised her hand and inquired what the coffee represented. The professor smiled. "I'm glad you asked. It just goes to show you that no matter how full your life may seem, there's always room for a couple of cups of coffee with a friend."

While you are focusing on getting out of debt, I hope you will remember to fill your jar with the important stuff! Good luck on your Debt Freedom March and God bless!

Wealthy Life Questions

1. Are you excited about your Debt Freedom March?

2. What specifically excites you up about this march?

Financial Education Is A Journey

"Success is not final, failure is not fatal; it is the courage to continue that counts."
WINSTON CHURCHILL

My number one goal in writing this book was to show you that you can get out of debt. However, one person alone cannot cover everything. After reading this book, I hope you are excited to learn and grow even more. Below are a list of books that have helped me greatly on my own financial and life journey.

For Financial Growth

The Automatic Millionaire: A Powerful One-Step Plan to Live and Finish Rich by David Bach

The Wealthy Barber by David Chilton

The Richest Man in Babylon by George Clason

Rich Habits - The Daily Success Habits of Wealthy Individuals by Thomas C. Corley

You Can Retire Sooner Than You Think by Wes Moss

The Total Money Makeover: Classic Edition: A Proven Plan for Financial Fitness by Dave Ramsey

Your Money or Your Life: 9 Steps to Transforming Your Relationship with Money and Achieving Financial Independence by Vicki Robin and Joe Dominguez

The Millionaire Next Door: The Surprising Secrets of America's Wealthy by Thomas J. Stanley and William D. Danko

For Personal Growth

Start: Punch Fear in the Face, Escape Average and Do Work that Matters by Jon Acuff

The Traveler's Gift: Seven Decisions that Determine Personal Success by Andy Andrews

The Alchemist by Paulo Coelho

The 7 Habits of Highly Effective People: Powerful Lessons in Personal Change by Stephen R. Covey

Start with Why: How Great Leaders Inspire Everyone to Take Action by Simon Sinek

Acknowledgements

Thank you God for giving me the gifts to help others handle their money better. I hope to continue using Your blessings to make this world a better place.

Tracy – Thank you so much for being the best wife and the best mommy to Ava and Ella. You use your gifts daily to make others have a better life and are the best person I know. You are my personal cheerleader. I am blessed to spend my life with you.

Ava and Ella – Thank you for being my daughters. I love being your daddy every single day and think both of you are amazing young ladies.

Mom - Thank you for the path you have set for me. You are the strongest woman I know and am blessed to have your guidance and love.

Nancy – WOW—my 4th book with you! Thank you for always being so supportive of me and my ideas. Words alone will never express how grateful I am for all you have done.

You – Thank you so much for taking time out of your busy schedule to read this book. Good luck on your Debt Freedom March. Please don't hesitate to reach out to me at www.wealthyteacher.weebly.com if I can ever be of further help to you. God bless!

ADDED BONUS! Visit my website and fill in the contact form—tell me where you bought this book and I will send you a free ebook, *How to Save $30,000 this Year.*

About The Author

Danny is currently a special education teacher in Georgia. He has also taught pre-k, kindergarten, first grade, second grade, and sixth grade.

In addition to this book, Danny is the author of four other personal finance books: *The Wealthy Teacher: Lessons for Prospering on a School Teacher's Salary*, *A Bright Financial Future: Teaching Kids About Money Pre-K through College for Life-Long Success*, *A Simple Book of Financial Wisdom: Teach Yourself (and Your Kids) How to Live Wealthy with Little Money* and *How To Survive (and perhaps thrive) On A Teacher's Salary*. When Danny's daughter, Ava, was nine years old, she also traditionally published her very own money book for kids, *The Financial Angel: What All Kids Should Know About Money (Ages 4-11)*.

Danny's everyday approach to handling money has led him to be interviewed on numerous television shows including Fox & Friends, The CBS Early Show, CNN's Newsroom, Fox News Channel's Happening Now, The 700 Club, The Clark Howard Show and MSNBC Live. He has also been interviewed on more than 650 radio shows and featured in numerous publications such as USA Today, Instructor Magazine, Woman's Day, Yahoo.com, The Wall Street Journal, Consumer Reports, Money Magazine and The Atlanta Journal Constitution. Danny wants to show others how to thrive on their salaries, too.

Learn more about Danny at
www.wealthyteacher.weebly.com

END NOTES

Author's Note

a. https://www.cnbc.com/2020/03/31/stock-market-today-live.html

b. https://tradingninvestment.com/stock-market-historical-returns/

c. https://www.investopedia.com/ask/answers/042415/what-average-annual-return-sp-500.asp

Preface

a. https://money.cnn.com/2018/05/22/pf/emergency-expenses-household-finances/index.html

b. https://www.marketwatch.com/story/a-growing-number-of-americans-have-more-credit-card-debt-than-savings-2019-02-13

c. https://www.nitrocollege.com/research/average-student-loan-debt

d. https://www.brides.com/gallery/american-wedding-study

Introduction

a. https://www.cnbc.com/2019/01/03/car-payments-and-loans-jump-amid-surging-demand-for-cars-suvs.html

Chapter 1

a. https://www.nerdwallet.com/blog/average-credit-card-debt-household/

b. https://www.usdebtclock.org/

c. http://www.cnn.com/2009/LIVING/02/04/trillion.dollars/

d. https://www.facebook.com/notes/dan-asmussen/what-a-trillion-dollars-looks-like-a-visualization-of-us-debt/10150303103185432

e. http://www1.cbn.com/guard-against-greed

f. https://www.redcrowmarketing.com/2015/09/10/many-ads-see-one-day/

g. http://www.investopedia.com/articles/financialcareers/10/buffett-frugal.asp

h. http://blogs.wsj.com/bankruptcy/2015/08/04/50-cent-bankruptcy-by-the-numbers/

i. https://www.bankrate.com/finance/celebrity-money/musicians-bankruptcy-tom-petty.aspx

j. http://usatoday30.usatoday.com/life/people/2004-04-26-don-johnson_x.htm

k. http://www.moneycrashers.com/bankrupt-celebrities-rich-broke/

l. https://www.thebalance.com/the-one-thing-most-millionaires-have-in-common-453694

m. https://www.inc.com/jt-odonnell/how-this-1-question-can-make-you-choose-wrong-career.html

Chapter 2

a. https://www.creditcards.com/credit-card-news/credit-card-vending-machines-increase-sales-1273.php#ixzz46DmkOHsH

b. https://www.nerdwallet.com/blog/credit-cards/credit-cards-make-you-spend-more/

c. https://www.everydayhealth.com/depression/the-link-between-depression-and-debt.aspx

d. https://www.thesimpledollar.com/the-emotional-effects-of-debt/

e. https://news.northwestern.edu/stories/2013/08/high-debt-could-be-hazardous-to-your-health

f. https://abcnews.go.com/Health/Wellness/ways-debt-bad-health/story?id=25066977

g. https://economix.blogs.nytimes.com/2009/12/07/money-fights-predict-divorce-rates/

h. https://budgeting.thenest.com/debt-affect-marriage-3238.html

i. https://phys.org/news/2013-07-reveals-early-financial-arguments-predictor.html

Chapter 3

a. https://disabilitycanhappen.org/disability-statistic/

b. https://en.wikipedia.org/wiki/Terri_Schiavo_case

c. https://www.foxbusiness.com/features/how-much-youre-losing-by-not-getting-your-employers-401k-match

d. https://www.bls.gov/news.release/hsgec.nr0.htm

e. https://www.jillonmoney.com/blog/tag/college+funding+vs+retirement

f. https://www.collegedata.com/en/pay-your-way/college-sticker-shock/how-much-does-college-cost/whats-the-price-tag-for-a-college-education/

Chapter 6

a. https://www.bankrate.com/banking/savings/financial-security-june-2018

Chapter 7

a. https://www.bls.gov/news.release/cesan.nr0.htm

b. https://taxfoundation.org/90-percent-taxpayers-projected-tcja-expanded-standard-deduction/

Chapter 8

a. https://www.nerdwallet.com/blog/loans/auto-loans/average-monthly-car-payment/

b.https://www.washingtonpost.com/news/wonk/wp/2015/08/28/americas-growing-love-affair-with-the-most-wasteful-thing-to-drink-there-is/?noredirect=on&utm_term=.9019b6072e4c

Scary Debt Statistics

http://www.theatlantic.com/magazine/archive/2016/05/my-secret-shame/476415/